Advanc

On Liking The Other: Queer Subjects And Religious Discourses

"Burke and Greteman have together done the apparently impossible. By refusing to accept the polarities either in their profession or our society, and approaching tense issues from the side, rather than head on, they have made possible an anthropology of teaching which is able to be simultaneously respectful and embracing of both queer and religious ways of being within the overall adventure of education. Loving, liking, considering, failing, forgiving, reconciling, and daring: each one of these is filled out and given a life-giving role in the way in which teaching leads us out and on."

—James Alison, Catholic Priest, Theologian and Author

"*On Liking the Other* explores sites of intersection and implication among three subjects—any of which are fraught with complexity and contestation taken alone: Queer Theory, Theology/Religion, and Teacher Education. Burke and Greteman give complicated depth to all three disciplines by noting their always, already entanglement. The authors eschew the obligatory, predictable, scathing indictments of religion that constitute an easy way. Instead, they invite us into the path of "liking," a middle way of relationship that topples our polarized entrenchments in love and hate. This, they suggest, is our best shot at real dialogue with one another. The book is smart, blessedly accessible—in short, brilliant. Read it."

—Ugena Whitlock, PhD, MDiv, Author, *This Corner of Canaan: Curriculum Studies of Place and the Reconstruction of the South*; Editor, *Queer South Rising: Voices of a Contested Place*; co-Editor, *Queer Studies and Education Series* (Palgrave Macmillan)

On Liking
The Other

QUEER SINGULARITIES:
LGBTQ HISTORIES, CULTURES, AND IDENTITIES IN EDUCATION SERIES

Dennis J. Sumara, PhD, Editor

Queer Singularities takes an intersectional approach to exploring how normative and non-normative experiences of gender, race, class, and sexuality are taught and learned within lesbian, gay, bisexual, transgendered, and queer histories, cultures, and identities.

Focused on processes and experiences of formal and informal education, books in the series will cover critical perspectives on topics such as schooling and sexuality, heteronormativity and learning, activism and curriculum, homophobia and trauma, urbanization and identity, and culture and creativity.

Through these exploratory juxtapositions, Queer Singularities aims to explore the paradoxical ways LGBTQ histories, cultures and identities are both productively singular and disruptively queer. In so doing, books in the series will provide new theoretical lenses and practical information for researchers, educators, leaders, and policy maker

Published and Forthcoming Titles:

Writing Beyond Recognition: Queer Re-Storying for Social Change
by Claire Robson (2021)

Our Children are Your Students: LGBTQ Families Speak Out
by Tara Goldstein (2021)

On Liking the Other: Queer Subjects and Religious Discourses
by Kevin J. Burke & Adam J. Greteman (2021)

The series editor, Dennis J. Sumara, PhD, invites individuals to submit proposals for any book-length manuscript, including but not restricted to the following:

- monographs
- textbooks
- edited collections
- primers
- readers
- anthologies
- handbooks
- conference proceedings

Prospectus guidelines can be found here: http://myersedpress.com/sites/stylus/ MEP/Docs/Prospectus%20Guidelines%20MEP.pdf. If you have a project that you wish to have considered for publication, please send a proposal, one or two sample chapters, and your current CV to: Chris Myers, Publisher, Myers Education Press (c.myers@myersedpress.com).

On Liking
The Other

Queer Subjects And Religious Discourses

BY *Kevin J. Burke & Adam J. Greteman*

Myers
Education
Press

Gorham, Maine

Published by Myers Education Press, LLC
P.O. Box 424, Gorham, ME 04038

Myers Education Press is an academic publisher specializing in books, e-books, and digital content in the field of education. All of our books are subjected to a rigorous peer review process and produced in compliance with the standards of the Council on Library and Information Resources.

Library of Congress Cataloging-in-Publication Data available from Library of Congress.

13-digit ISBN 978-1-9755-0407-6 (paperback)
13-digit ISBN 978-1-9755-0408-3 (library networkable e-edition)
13-digit ISBN 978-1-9755-0409-0 (consumer e-edition)

Printed in the United States of America.

All first editions printed on acid-free paper that meets the American National Standards Institute Z39-48 standard.

Books published by Myers Education Press may be purchased at special quantity discount rates for groups, workshops, training organizations, and classroom usage. Please call our customer service department at 1-800-232-0223 for details.

Cover design by Teresa Lagrange

Visit us on the web at **www.myersedpress.com** to browse our complete list of titles.

DEDICATION

This book is dedicated to teacher educators and student teachers who stay with the trouble and lean into complicated conversations, particularly, but not limited to, those at the heart of this book around sexualities, genders, and religions as they enter classrooms. The work of teacher education is challenging as it encounters a range of ever-changing and complex realities, identities, and practices. We have immense gratitude for those in our lives who have engaged us in the difficult conversations necessary to produce work that we like. In particular, we are grateful to our families as well as to our shared teachers: Avner Segall, Lynn Fendler, Cleo Cherryholmes, and James Alison.

Contents

Acknowledgments

This tends to be as much a space of forgetting as it is acknowledging, which is to say that nearly every author that we've read—and even we as authors in the past ourselves—is at pains to note that although they have remembered the aid of a great many people (and perhaps nonpeople) in the writing of a given book, they will certainly have forgotten some, not out of callousness but out of the failings of memory. So be it. We are grateful to Dennis Sumara for the opportunity to join his wonderful *Queer Singularities* series, just as we're grateful to Chris Myers and the staff at Myers Education Press for their generosity and patience as this book took longer than it ought to have given the state of the world in 2020 and 2021 when we wrote it. We're glad of the many conversation partners we've found at conferences, in courses (our students most especially), and, most particularly, through the writings that have shaped our thinking. And finally, we're deeply indebted to our families for their support throughout our careers generally but, most especially, regarding this book, which has been percolating for the better part of a decade now.

Toward Pedagogies of Liking

Dennis Sumara, Series Editor

IT IS LATE April, 1966 and I am seven years old eavesdropping on the suddenly heated conversation between my recently widowed mother and the Catholic priest who had stopped by our tiny 1950s bungalow to offer condolences and prayers. They are in the Living Room, a place reserved for special company and the RCA Victor Hi-Fi that played my mother's Maria Callas and Dean Martin records. There is no music that day, only the determined German accented English overriding any attempts at prayers by the priest. Mrs. Sumara is not interested in prayers it seems. She wants to know what else the church can do to help with her suddenly desperately-poor-with-no-family-to-speak-of situation. Apparently not much. My mother never set foot in a Catholic church again, making her Dream Book, which she consulted most mornings, a replacement for her Bible.

I remember missing the ritual, not only of the Catholic "High Mass" with chanting, incense, holy water, and hymns—but also how Sunday morning became a special time. There were rituals about what we ate, how we dressed for church, what we did after Sunday Mass. Plenty of ceremony and spectacle followed by drives to the nearby Rocky Mountains to pick wild mushrooms in the forest and eat potato salad and ham buns by a lake or creek. The perfect perceptual education for an emerging queer kid who learned to play the accordion, watched The Carol Burnett Show every week, danced to disco music in the 70s, and was mentored into the queer community by drag queens.

Many years later, near the end of her life, my mother told me she missed Sunday Mass, but could not reconcile that fondness for things about the church she no longer liked. Now that I am as old as she was when she uttered those words,

I know that it is sometimes easier to feel "love" than to cultivate the reliable attachment of "like." As Burke and Greteman express so eloquently in this volume, "liking" needs to be learned. To learn to like might even need a curriculum and some pedagogy. Learning to like might be a singularly queer education.

These are the sorts of singular ironic paradoxes that are explored in the *Queer Singularities* book series. Focused on processes and experiences of formal and informal education, books in the series offer critical perspectives on topics such as schooling and sexuality, heteronormativity and learning, activism and curriculum, homophobia and trauma, urbanization and identity, culture and creativity—and, with this volume, one that I could not have predicted when I conceptualized the series—queer and religious discourses.

The ongoing and at times and places amplified antagonisms between religious and queer discourses are what Freud (1929) conceptualizes as narcissisms of minor differences to explain inter-group antagonisms, which are always played out through the individual. The seeming impasses between queer gender and sexuality histories, cultures and identities and those of religion can seem incommensurable. Freud argued that in order for a person to maintain a coherent self-identity, a certain degree of narcissism must be developed. This narcissism, he suggested, is supported by the *learned* ability to make distinctions between oneself and others–to notice minor differences and to make them matter. Of course, we each pay a psychic price for group membership, since we must turn the desire to conform against our individuality (Sumara, 2007). At some point, however, decisions have to be made about how much eccentricity to allow into one's daily performance of self-identity—a tension between what I have described as "the fear of being ordinary and the desire to belong" (Sumara, forthcoming). And therein lies the problem: those narcissisms of minor differences, once regulated into a the normal/not normal binary become obviously and necessarily oppositional.

On Liking the Other resists attempts to essentialize subjects or subjectivities, nor does it make easy moves to the polemical or conclusive. Instead it brings the reader into the kind of complicated curriculum conversation that William Pinar (1975) initiated nearly 50 years ago when he noted that the curriculum emerges from the Latin *currere*—literally, the running of the course. Like Pinar, in this volume Burke and Greteman have made that path more vibrant and, in some ways, more difficult for the reader by ensuring a rich and sometimes unexpected juxtaposing of ideas and discourses, provoking us to not only consider the possibilities, but also the urgent necessities of learning to like the other. I know that I am reconsidering the lines I have drawn, a sure sign that I have just read a great book, one that I predict will condition the pedagogical provocations needed in all places of teaching and learning.

References

Freud, S. (1929). *Civilization and its discontents.* Pelican.

Pinar, W. (1975). (Ed.). *Curriculum theorizing: The reconceptualists.* McCutchan.

Sumara, D. (2007) Small Differences Matter: Interrupting Certainty About Identity in Teacher Education, *Journal of Gay & Lesbian Issues in Education,* 4:4, 39-58.

Sumara, D. (Forthcoming). Reading My Queer Archive of Deferrals. In D. Sumara & D. Alvermann (Eds). *Ideas that changed literacy practices: First person accounts from leading voices.* Myers Educational Press.

Clearing The Ground

WE WRITE THIS book as we—two scholars who are similarly interested in the challenges and opportunities that exist when "queer" meets "Christian" in teacher education. Both terms, we admit, immediately get complicated, potentially raising hackles and setting off warning bells for students and teachers alike. What good can come of exploring possible meetings between "queer" and "Christian" in teacher education when the terms, related histories, and practices are so often at odds? When so often this chiasmus is rooted in pain experienced by bodies that inhabit queer, inhabit Christian, and have different—and valid or not—claims to persecution at the hands of the other? We cannot and will not directly address such claims—real or perceived—as we suspect such claims need to be assessed in their contexts and conditions. For some, on either side, this might sound dangerous, perhaps ludicrous, because of the evidence; the evidence they will say. But ours is not a concern to litigate such matters, although litigation is explored in Chapter 4. Rather, ours is a concern with telling a different story about such meetings. Scholars—notably historians and theologians—have already illustrated that the stories that have been told about "homosexuality" and Christianity, for instance, are more complex than often popularly understood. Such scholarship is important to us because it lays the groundwork for recognizing different possibilities at the juncture point. Our concern, instead, is to think about how those terms—their histories and practices—meet in teacher education classrooms—sometimes quite visibly, other times less so. What is true, we want to suggest broadly, is that when they meet, more often than not, teacher educators and student teachers are less than confident as to how to proceed. After all, both terms have a complex and intimate history within education: Christianity always present in the bones, the structures, the practices that make up public schools; queer, always feared for the ways the nonnormative—shape-shifting over time—is excluded from the work of creating "citizens" and "families."

Yet these histories do not determine our futures, but they surely shape our current conditions. More recent educational histories show the ways demographic shifts have expanded who is included and what is included in a social vision of schooling, allowing for continued, if different, curriculum questions about "worth." We suspect it is worth our time to contemplate telling new stories—rooted both in "queer" and "Christian," more specifically, Catholic, ideas—that make for more interesting meetings that might, just might, allow for change moments in teacher education classrooms to learn different lessons, lessons that might shape student teachers' own future students who will, themselves, remix and tell anew stories at the intersection of, more broadly, "religion" and "queerness."

In his later work, the curriculum theorist James B. Macdonald (1995) asserted that because "curriculum theory is an ever renewing attempt to interpret curricular reality . . . to develop greater understanding," it is best to think of the "act of theorizing" as "an act of faith" particularly because it is an assertion of belief that, and here he draws on William James, "necessitates an act of the moral will" such that curriculum theorizing might better be understood as a "prayerful act" in the direction of a more humanizing vision of life in the world (p. 181). One of the assertions that we make at the front end here is that although religion might seem irrelevant to, if not explicitly counterposed with, more progressive orientations to gender and sexuality in schools, the reality of lived experience, as well as with faith and theology, tells a much more interesting and nuanced story. That is, that if a kind of defensiveness emerges when encountering the assertion that theory, for instance, could require an act of faith or be couched in the language of prayerfulness, we ought to linger with that reaction. This is not our attempt at constructing a straw person out of the reader; certainly, there are reasons to be cautious with religious language, weaponized as it has often been—and often still is—against gender and sexual diversity. Rather our baseline assertion is that a great deal of possibility is lost in the absence of engagement with religious discourses from reparative positions. It is the case that theology, furthermore, has much to say about human (and divine, of course) creativity, engagement, and, ultimately, education with which the social sciences might do new work. One way to think of this is that theology is an epistemology through which we might think old problems anew if we, in educational research, and, in this book, specifically teacher education, engage it seriously rather than solely with suspicion. To think with mystery, or around concepts of grace or amid the inherently queer bodily manifestations present in much of Christian religious representation (to say nothing of other religious traditions) is to work in exactly the kind of complicated conversation that best colors critical work in educational research. We hope to find the shape of a new story in our work here.

Telling new stories is not merely to tell them but to also recognize how they open up new ways for teachers and students to encounter one another. School is, after all, a key institution where people meet and encounter one another and bodies of knowledge. We can think perhaps most easily about not only students encountering one another and their teachers but also the ways parents are part of un/balancing the equation. So, too, we should recognize how students and teachers encounter the legacies that inform the functioning of schools, most easily seen through the legacies of legislation and judicial decisions. The histories of American public education and higher education are filled with stories of exclusion and the struggle for inclusion. This is true for both religious teachers and students—individuals for whom religious identity is central to a sense of self and family—and LGBTQ+ teachers and students—individuals for whom sexual and gender identities are central to a sense of self and community.

LGBTQ+ students and teachers, in particular, have struggled for a place in the classroom for decades. As Lugg (2016) argues, there has been a persistent refusal to include LGBTQ+ educators because of the pernicious legacies of homophobia—notably "recruitment" myths—and the formative nature of education. LGBTQ+ educators are surely more visible in the 21st century, and their legal rights to employment were affirmed with the Supreme Court's 2020 decision in *Bostock v. Clayton County*, which barred employment discrimination based on sexual orientation and gender identity. Yet legal protections only provide a framework in which to exist while the everyday challenges of navigating school remain ever present. LGBTQ+ students have perhaps fared slightly better given gains in not only antibullying and harassment policies enumerating sexual orientation and gender identity but also the court's continued confirmation of LGBTQ+ students' rights to assemble (Gay/Straight Alliances) and evolving legislation mandating curricular inclusion of LGBTQ+ histories. Even so, such gains centralize a rights framework that narrowly construes these issues, often foregoing conversations about freedom. Put differently, drawing on Jakobsen and Pellegrini (2004), the emphasis on rights protecting subjects against discrimination neglects the need to be actively *for* freedom. Still, to be for freedom raises challenges made visible around calls for religious freedom alongside calls for sexual freedom, calls that are not new but have long histories.

Amid the founding of American public schools and their expansion in the early 20th century, key battles took place impacting the place of religion—notably Protestantism—and the demands by Catholics either for public funding for their schools or freedom from partisan religious curricula in public ones. Vestiges of these battles remain into the 21st century as debates about public funding of private and religious schools persist, alongside arguments allowing students to "opt out" due to religious objections. The anchor in the arguments, however, is "the embrace of hopefulness" that pervades public schooling in the United States, which continually reinforces "the old assumption that schools were [and are still] fundamental to individual and social betterment" (Reese, 2005, p. 2018). This "educationalizing" of "social problems" (Labaree, 2010, p. 243) has made schooling "the answer to social problems" as well as its failure to do so "an indispensable political tool" (p. 232). What Labaree argues is that the consistent failure of public education in America to enable us to achieve our highest intentions is both inevitable and politically useful; it's not accidental, and the best we might hope for is to hold "the school system responsible for expressing our values rather than for actually realizing them in practice" (p. 234). The tortured question, of course, surrounds the "our" from which these values might be drawn, which is part of what we're thinking with here; we don't rightly know, but we do know that the aporia that says schools are responsible for the ethical uplift of students even if they can't guarantee it outlines the very tension of what we're doing all the time in teacher education. The diversity of the bodies that represent the values that fall under the category of "our" is precisely what we need to think about and with.

This diverse set of bodies is made visible through litigation and attempts to regulate what teachers and students can or cannot do or be made to do within public schools. This regulation has been nowhere more present and contentious than around religion. As Justin Driver (2018) argues, "beginning in the early 1960s, the Court held that the First Amendment's prohibition on establishing religion barred public school educators from leading their pupils in religious exercises" (p. 362). Teachers have limits on what, in terms of religious discourses and practices, they can bring into explicit practice in their classrooms. And the court's opinions, as Driver continues,

> demonstrate awareness both that the public school setting poten-
> tially imposes acute coercive pressure on students' religious beliefs
> and that this religiously diverse nation must take special steps to
> forestall any notion that simply receiving an education subjects
> students to proselytization. (pp. 362–363)

Although students generally have diminished rights and protections within schools, under the Establishment Clause of the First Amendment, the court has consistently provided students with "enhanced protections" (Driver, 2018, p. 363). Laws, of course, as we explore in a later chapter, are limited in their ability to address real-world inequities precisely because they fall short of the Law as Platonic form. That is, although there are legal limits on religious practices in classrooms, we will always fail to eliminate, with the juridical, the actual practice of religion as it is made manifest by religious and areligious bodies in a given space. We all, in other words, bear the traces of religion—even if our orientation is fundamentally to resist religion—because of the way in which, particularly in an American context, education remains imbued with Christian religious intentions, discourses, language, and adherents. Or, as Melissa Sanchez (2019) reminds us,

> while it is empirically true that organized religion's formal role in
> the state has been restricted in modern Western societies, from
> French *laïcité* to the US separation of church and state, it is also
> true that Christian perspectives and practices still inform everyday
> life and state politics in a myriad of norms so taken for granted that
> their credal basis has been rendered all but invisible. (p. 9)

What are we to do, then, with the religious as it enters our classrooms? And what are we to do when it enters in ways that are at odds with other commitments and ways of living and being in the world? We are not convinced that we can offer answers to these questions or a new principle to stand on but hope to respond to such challenges in ways that story into possibility new ways of encountering differences.

This is, bluntly, not a book that will offer principles to stand on or by that err to one side or the other. Ours is not a principled stance. "Sometimes," Andrew Koppelman (2020) reminds us, "the right thing to do is not to follow principle, but to accurately discern the interests at stake and cobble together an approach that gives some weight to each of those interests" (p. 4). While for some, cobbling together an approach might seem a cop-out, hobbling principled causes, we suspect that teaching on the ground, in classrooms, is always an act of cobbling together ways to engage the diverse bodies and ideas that present themselves to be part of educational conversations. Such conversations are ever changing and often quickly complicated by the legacies that are embodied not only by students who have experienced school in all kinds of ways but also by teachers who themselves were once students, who encountered school and its practices.

On Conversation

In this book, we centralize the work of conversation. We, at the start of each chapter, except Chapter 1, offer a preliminary conversation between the two of us that separates out our two voices, which will otherwise be merged, hopefully successfully, into a singular shared voice. These preliminary conversations are to make visible some of the "background conversations" that led to each particular chapter and to bring a certain "conversational" tone into the work. It is, in a sense, our attempt to show the cobbling we do as teachers and scholars. We think scholarship emerges, in large part, through conversations fostered in various contexts, alongside the work we do as individuals in the solitude of our own spaces. As coauthors, there are moments in every chapter when we take on a topic as individuals, but such work is still always in conversation with the other. This collaboration is made manifest through editing, asking questions in pursuit of clarification, and building off the established writing in a given draft. Combined, we hope these preliminary conversations provide an "in" to the work along with insight into our purpose and interests for each chapter. We bring different commitments to this work that will, we hope, allow us to create a multivocal text that shows both our shared and separate ideas alongside one another. We also hope, to reiterate, they will show how ideas emerge through conversation, are developed, reworked, and offered to readers to do with what they will. We hope this is helpful to make transparent our process while also providing different ways into the constellation of issues we take up to cobble together an approach to these matters of concern.

We seek, in conversation, to do something else, perhaps more mundane: to come to different, maybe new, understandings of shared topics and/or curiosities together. Here we are curious about religion, sexuality, and gender as they present challenges within teacher education and thus education more generally. There is a rich texture to the art of conversations. A conversation is, at its heart, an exchange of ideas. Yet such an exchange is fraught with histories of what conversation has historically sought to do. A conversation is, after all, etymologically tied to the work of conversion, a religious act (and, historically, often a violent act). Acts of conversion, when turned outward, are rooted in conversations with an other in the hope that the "other" will become like one's self, converted to one's side or one's beliefs. In becoming like one's self, the other is erased. Like-mindedness prevails. Such acts of conversion are, in the West, tied to histories of colonialism, homophobia, and nationalism that inflict shame, violence, and erasure on those, queer, non-Christian, non-White "others" toward which they are oriented.

Still, etymology is not destiny. As Jane Roland Martin (1985) suggests,

> a good conversation is neither a fight nor a contest. Circular in form, cooperative in nature, and constructive in intent, it is an interchange of ideas by those who see themselves not as adversaries but as human beings come together to talk and listen and learn from one another. (p. 10)

Recognizing the tenuousness of the conversation and its related uses, we seek to redeem conversation as an art that allows for new ideas to emerge amid the (heated) exchange. The work of conversation is one engaged in quite often with those one likes, but the intentions of such conversations are not to cultivate like-mindedness. Conversation, ours here in particular, is not, we hope, an attempt to "meet" in the middle and adjudicate between two viewpoints. Nor is it an attempt to "agree to disagree." Rather, it is an attempt to stay with the trouble of the problem at hand to create different modes and models for meeting others who always already are implicated in religious and queer discourses. As

American composer Jonathan Larson (Larson et al., 1997) wrote in the song "La Vie Boheme," "the opposite of war isn't peace. . . . It's creation." At first glance, religious and queer discourses have long been at war; our understanding of this relationship may rest on the assumption that this is the only story to tell. Upon additional encounters, we hope to productively illustrate how there are actually ways to make peace at the intersection here, in search of something different out of which we might create anew.

Many of these issues and their intersections have instantiated a range of controversies that provoke court cases, culture wars, and more. Rather than rehashing those controversies along already-established camps, we seek to move to the side of controversy to offer different ways into the work that can happen when "queer" and "religion" meet. This is, as you will see throughout, hesitant work as we recognize the complicated and often traumatic histories that are implicated. So we hedge; we question; we express uncertainty. This is out of a sincere hope, a critical hope perhaps, that such hesitations allow for a different story to emerge that recognizes the resonances and nuances that are often present alongside controversy, just less likely to create headlines.

A Preliminary Conversation

Adam: I think it might be useful at the outset to document why this book and why now. Books after all do not just emerge out of nowhere. Rather, they emerge through, at least in my experience, angst, confusions, and conversations with others in particular contexts and conditions. Those others are both colleagues and friends, as well as students we teach and other scholars and researchers who we take up and read. There are also those with whom we might vehemently disagree or whose ideas we find problematic on various accounts that inevitably seep into our minds, asking for our consideration. Amid such work, ideas begin to take form and, in some circumstances, become more fully fleshed out into a possible book. It is a long and winding process with detours and roadblocks. This being particularly true in the thick of a global public health pandemic (COVID-19) that not only disrupted so many aspects of our lives but also laid bare any number of material realities for each of us in different ways.

For me, this book comes at a moment in which the tensions between the rights and freedoms of LGBTQ+[1] persons and religious rights and freedom are front and center, exacerbated, in part, by the administration of Donald J. Trump. For instance, toward the end of writing the book, about 30 current students and alums of evangelical colleges sued the U.S. Department of Education over religious exemptions provided by law to religious schools. Their argument is that such exemptions fail to protect LGBTQ+ students against discrimination; this a violation of Title IX (Redden, 2021). The lawyer representing the students, Paul Carlos Southwick, argued, "The government is actually giving its stamp of approval to the discrimination through its federal funding. That is a violation of the due process rights and equal protection rights of LGBTQ students" (Redden, 2021, para. 4). Continuing, Southwick stated, "The Supreme Court has made clear that the government can no longer treat gay people in a manner that fails to recognize their dignity as human beings" (Redden, 2021, para. 4).

The Council of Christian Colleges and Universities (CCCU; 2021), in a statement after the suit was filed, noted:

> CCCU institutions should be places where all students feel safe, supported, and welcome. We know the college experience can be stressful, and even more so for LGBTQ students who are working to understand how their sexual orientation or gender identity intersects with their personal faith. (para. 3)

Continuing, it said:

> CCCU institutions serve diverse student bodies and work to care for all students. There is zero tolerance for bullying, harassment, and assault at CCCU institutions, and campus leaders understand their responsibility to ensure that all students believe and feel that they are created in the image of God and therefore possess full dignity, value, and worth. (CCCU, 2021, para. 4)

The outcome of this case is not known at the time of writing, but it touches on the tensions that exist as educational institutions, student bodies, and federal policies come head to head with competing interests and ideologies.

Such legal battles can often seem, to some extent, quite removed from the everyday as these issues are argued in the courts around particular instances with specific litigants. But those arguments filter down and into the everyday lives of, for us, student teachers and teacher educators for whom questions of sexuality, gender identity, and religious identity are worn into educational spaces. The legal cases may be battled and will take time to unfold, but the time of the courts does not allow for schooltime as educators and students continue their work of teaching and learning. This leaves students and teachers, particularly those who embody, for instance, LGBTQ+ religious identities, with the task of navigating not only their identities but also if/how those identities play out with those around them in classrooms and school communities.

This navigation is seemingly rarely engaged, educationally, out in the open. Rather, such issues are navigated individually, on our own, or in hushed side conversations with like-minded folks. If it does rear its head in the space and time of class, it often becomes quickly politicized with sides immediately set. This is not, of course, entirely true as it is probably the politicized moments that get airtime with headlines about gay teachers being fired, new data about bullying rooted in homo- and transphobia, or stories about Christian students being silenced or Islamic or Jewish students encountering forms of anti-Semitism or Islamophobia. Moments in which sexuality, gender identity, and religion meet each play out in different ways and provoke various forms of political commentary, questioning, for instance, the veracity of claims of victimization (do White Christian students experience persecution?) or the extent of the problem (have LGBTQ+ people made progress on the rights front?).

There are, I have to imagine, examples of how such navigation happens in ways that do justice to the complex realities in play. Yet those examples rarely make headlines because they don't offer splashy sound bites. Instead, such moments stay with the trouble involved and the complex issues in play. They, in a sense, cobble together an approach, maybe even leaving principles behind. I hope that part of this work allows us to imagine ways and practices that might help, in particular, teacher educators navigate conversations with student teachers that raise sticky issues around sexuality, gender, and religion. After all, such ways and practices can inform how those student teachers engage such issues with their own future students and colleagues. And I want to imagine that doing so with an eye to both "theological" and "queer" languages will provide ways into such conversations that recognize the different but related ways both discourses work toward similar relations.

Kevin: Some of this is not only strictly utilitarian but also perhaps useful to reveal to the reader and especially early-career scholars who wonder about the move from idea to book. My brother-in-law, who is a scholar of social studies education and who attended Michigan State with Adam and me, told me early in our shared careers, that he always said yes to requests to conduct peer review for journals because it meant he got to learn something new, each time, about where the field was moving. I followed that particular koan-ic approach to reviewing for the first 10 years of my career and then got a bit more judicious amid the pandemic for purely practical reasons: The 5- and 7-year-old, quarantined, demanded more immediate attention than the blinded article. What remains, however, is the idea of saying yes to opportunities, which is rooted in a kind of neediness that emerges from a particular White, straight, middle-class "achievement" upbringing, much like what comes from Lareau's (2003) "concerted cultivation." But there's also a deep element of FOMO (fear of missing out) motivating things as well as an insecurity about academic life, even a pretty secure one, that tells me to accept all invitations. That is a long way of saying that a colleague asked me to lunch because she thought I should meet Dennis Sumara, the editor of this book series. This book is a result of that midwinter lunch, although Adam and I had bounced the ideas around for a while and were working on the prospectus for the thing, admittedly without a particular direction in relation to publication. We were being dilatory about it, which is often what conversation needs: the ground tilled, seeds scattered until it needs to be moved forward, actively cultivated, lest it fail to germinate.

The longer tale, however, is that Adam and I have always wandered a bit on the edges of religion in relation to queer theory. Certainly, we've written about it together elsewhere and productively, although not without resistance, particularly at the level of peer review: As hard as it is to find reviewers in general, it's near impossible to find reviewers in education who are conversant enough in theology to confidently evaluate such work. One version of that is, well, that's because theology isn't relevant to our work, so it ought to be tossed aside. My sense, however, is that we're missing rich ways of thinking the world anew if we ignore it, most especially because of how frequently religion, driven by interesting or damaging or limited theology, follows our teacher education students into our, and subsequently their, classrooms. And so I've spent more time recently reading theology because I think there are implications for *public* education that we've been willfully ignoring for the better part of the last 70 years; that's not a monolith, of course; there are people who do the work, and we cite them later. But I suppose I wonder just what we might do that's helpful if, as Adam suggests above, we mirror St. Augustine who came to Christianity, supposedly, after hearing the call "tolle lege"—take up and read—from just beyond his sightline.

A central concept that we have engaged previously and will turn to again here is that of "liking." It is a rather mundane concept and perhaps one that has amid the 21st century become ubiquitous. Yet, amid all the liking, we want to suggest that liking the other leaves space for the other to exist as other. Unlike love, which can quickly become conditional, and hate, which so often seeks to eliminate the other, like asks us to feel something else.

Adam: This something else is related to the work of coming into presence differently. A central purpose for education—as various scholars such as Hannah Arendt and Gert Biesta have argued—is the work of bringing subjects into presence or "subjectification." Through not only schools but through families and friendships, we come into presence: making sense of a self that will itself change. The self that comes into presence is not merely a replica of what selves have been in the past, nor is it completely divorced from the world it was born into. Rather, the self comes into presence amid the dynamic interplay of ideas, discourses, practices, bodies, and more. However, this work of coming into presence is never-ending; it is an incessant becoming. This becoming is, we suspect, impacted by education, as well as religious institutions, family, and media. But it is the self—the subject—that inevitably comes into presence. "What is at stake in the idea of subjectification," for Biesta (2020), "is our freedom as human beings and, more specifically, our freedom to act or to refrain from action" (p. 93). This is, in his estimation, an existential matter "about how I exist as the subject of my own life, not as the object of what other people want from me." Of course, other people—teachers included—often want things from students. The key, however, is to maintain an eye toward the uniqueness of students as subjects coming into presence who may very well disappoint in their becoming, but such disappointment might just say more about a teacher than it does about a student working to become a self.

Kevin: We note this elsewhere as well, but there will be slippage in the terms we use. This is a product of our shared writing process, as well as our fairly heterogeneous reading practices. It also could be chalked up to a kind of carelessness that readers might find frustrating or, we hope, a bit freeing. And so here we use, for instance, *religion, theology,* and, less frequently, *spirituality* to indicate loosely configured concepts and fields generally understudied in queer social science spaces for their *possibility*. Certainly, we might differentiate religion, as an adherence to a specific doctrine within a given denomination, from theology, the scholarly underpinnings for religious belief as further distinguished from spirituality. This last seems often like a kind of faith experienced by an individual, drifting in more progressive circles toward mysticism if not agnosticism. Our task in the book is to try to encounter religion, its theologies, and the faith lives of teachers, teacher candidates, and students anew. Most frequently, because of our shared histories, we write from Christian religious standpoints. This is a limitation of the work and one that should be held onto by the reader we hope in good faith (pun intended) but also as a sign that more work could be done and that our biases are always with us in our writing and thus further written into the very archives of our research.

Feeling Into Reason

Our work here emerged by feeling our way into the challenges, complexities, and conundrums that we noticed in not only our own teaching practices in teacher education but also scholarship within education and elsewhere in the humanities and social sciences. Issues within classrooms prompted questions about how to not only engage students with scholarship that might help them join conversations that preceded them but also grapple with the ways classrooms are implicated in helping students see (or not see) themselves in the curriculum. All of this, of course, with an eye toward the reality that our students will (potentially) be tomorrow's teachers. So our practices need to be held under a microscope as well to see if and how they live up to our own "talk": turning our abstract commitments to, for instance, critical inquiry, to justice, to antihomophobia, to antiracism, to equality, to ethics into concrete practices.

Implicated in this work are feelings: feelings not to be overcome and avoided but rather engaged and explored for what they can teach us in such work. At various points in the evolution of this book, both of us encountered a range of feelings—some shared and others not—that both inspired writing and thwarted it. For instance, given the history and current manifestations of homophobia in the Catholic Church, Adam struggled with the viability of such a project, unsure if he could, in good conscience, handle when "queer" and "religion" meet since such meetings seem more violent than not. This reality was made visible, for instance, in March 2021 when the Congregation for the Doctrine of the Faith (CDF)—the doctrinal watchdog of the Vatican—announced that priests were not allowed to bless same-sex marriages, although such blessings have been offered in lieu of marriage (Puella, 2021). Yet such announcements are not surprising; rather, they provoke feelings of disappointment, feelings felt in the gut. These gut feelings provided, however, evidence that such work was probably necessary so such feelings don't go to waste, don't fester unengaged. Feelings—of fear, of disgust, of disappointment—became part of the reason to continue the work to see what such feelings lead us toward.

The work as you will read in the coming chapters is not certain. We are, to reiterate, hesitant and hedge our arguments more than some might like. We have, as collaborators, received a fair share of reviews over the years pointing out our tendency to hedge. Our hedging is often seen as a confidence problem, a problem in believing in our argument or believing in ourselves. Yet we are not sure hesitancy and hedging indicate a lack of confidence. In this book in particular, we are quite certain that remaining uncertain or hesitant is central to the work of not only clearing some ground to allow for these conversations but also in attempting to build different educational conversations and practices amid polarized and, at times, at least at first blush, diametrically opposed positions. Such positions are, of course, always more than meets the eye as people who take such positions can quickly be revealed or exposed to be more complicated and complex. These moments can often confirm the other side's suspicions, pointing out, for instance, hypocrisy. But what if there could be other ways of not only taking positions that don't require certainty or only fellow feeling but also recognizing the importance of uncertainty and bad feelings in such conversations and how we accompany one another in navigating them?

Bad feelings—feelings like rage or anger—have an important role in this work given the histories such feelings have played when queer and religion meet. There are reasons to be angry, and anger is often quite reasonable. Marilyn Frye (1983) argues that "anger is always righteous." "To be angry," she continues, "you have to have some sense of the rightness or propriety of your position and your interest in whatever has been hindered, interfered with or harmed and anger implies a claim to such righteousness or propriety" (p. 86). This is a uniquely religious concept as well. Blumenthal (1993) writes of the dialectic of power, between humans and God, in a post-Holocaust world in which it is revealed in personalist theological circles that although "God's power is absolute . . . God cannot use it absolutely (p. 16). As such, in the Hebrew scriptures, when "God gets angry" out of a "righteous indignation," such anger is "rooted in covenant and, because covenant is rooted in mutuality, humans have space to rage at God, too" (p. 17). Thus, we find numerous psalms that involve lamentations at the failings of God in the world just as we find, for instance, entire theological traditions like feminist strands that emerged from Mary Daly (1973) and others that understand that "the entire conceptual systems of theology and ethics" unless critiqued and redeveloped through particularist stances (queer ones, Black ones, Indigenous ones, etc.) will remain wholly "developed under the conditions of patriarchy" as they "tend to serve the interests of sexist society" (p. 4). Anger is appropriate, and we can engage it from many places, including religious anger about the limitations of religion. We not only accept this wholeheartedly but also recognize that multiple sides representing diverse positions claim anger righteously, requiring that we either litigate whose anger is right and proper and whose anger bears false witness or stay with the trouble such anger raises to see if, perhaps, we can get to the matters that concern those involved.

As teacher educators, thinking specifically about the contingent and changing dynamics of classroom life in this book, we want to suggest that we need to make different gestures toward these differences and controversies that don't offer certainty but take comfort in the need for uncertainty, for hesitancy. Our hesitancy should not be taken as a wish to avoid conflict. Rather, it is an opening to engage in such meetings with a recognition that conflict is central to teaching and learning. Sarah Schulman (2016), in her aptly titled *Conflict Is Not Abuse*, not only points out the importance of being able to distinguish between conflict and abuse but also points to practices that grapple with conflict. In particular,

Schulman returns to practices rooted in community and the potential for re-storative practices that avoid institutions like the police and courts. Abuse, as a framing device, often defined many stories told about and between religion and sexuality discourses. Abuse frames the relations and in an array of documented cases, such as child sexual abuse and the abuse of nuns, abuse is the correct frame. Yet we are interested in moments that are conflictual, not abusive or merely controversial. Conflict is, as Schulman argued, not abuse. And this asks that we contemplate ways through such conflict educationally, rooted in our re-sponsibility to our learning communities, so such conflicts are not perennially reproduced or simply ignored but allowed to take us elsewhere.

Endnotes

1 As a general rule in the text, we use LGBTQ+ recognizing that the acronym is additive and expanding. Of course, there exist a number of permutations of the acronym, and these permutations themselves change over time and use. This changing and expansive reality of the LGBTQ+ acronym is one of the central pertinent issues that emerges in queer theoretical reflections on identity positions: They shift and resist permanence. Occasionally in the text, where we are quot-ing other sources or referring to texts that use other designations, we adjust the acronym without comment. This is to recognize not only that the acronym can function as an umbrella that inevitably fails to capture everyone but that, at times, it also operates to address specific identities under that umbrella.

References

Biesta, G. (2020). Risking ourselves in education: Qualification, socialization, and subjectification revisited. *Educational Theory, 70*(1), 89-104

Blumenthal, D. R. (1993). *Facing the abusing god: A theology of protest.* John Knox Press.

Council for Christian Colleges and Universities. (2021, April 1). *CCCU statement on law-suit filed against Department of Education.* https://www.cccu.org/news-updates/cccu-statement-lawsuit-filed-department-education/

Daly, M. (1973). *Beyond God the father: Toward a philosophy of women's liberation.* Bea-con Press.

Driver, J. (2018). *The schoolhouse gate: Public education, the supreme court, and the battle for the American mind.* Pantheon.

Frye, M. (1983). *The politics of reality.* The Crossing Press.

Jakobsen, J. R., & Pellegrini, A. (2004). *Love the sin: Sexual regulation and the limits of religious tolerance*. Beacon Press.

Koppelman, A. (2020). *Gay rights vs. religious liberty: The unnecessary conflict*. Oxford University Press.

Labaree, D. F. (2010). *Someone has to fail: The zero-sum game of public schooling*. Harvard University Press.

Lareau, A. (2003). *Unequal childhoods: Class, race, and family life*. University of California Press.

Larson, J., McDonnell, E., & Silberger, K. (1997). *Rent*. HarperEntertainment/HarperCollins.

Lugg, C.A. (2016). U.S. public schools and the politics of queer erasure. Palgrave Macmillan

Macdonald, J. B. (1995). *Theory as a prayerful act: The collected essays of James B. Macdonald* (B. J. Macdonald, Ed.). Peter Lang.

Martin, J. R. (1985). *Reclaiming a conversation: The ideal of the educated woman*. Yale University Press.

Puella, P. (2021, March 15). *In setback for gay Catholics, Vatican says church cannot bless same-sex unions*. Reuters. https://www.reuters.com/article/us-vatican-lgbt/in-setback-for-gay-catholics-vatican-says-church-cannot-bless-same-sex-unions-idUSKBN2B71C3

Redden, E. (2021, April 6). Religious freedom vs. freedom from discrimination. *Inside Higher Ed*. https://www.insidehighered.com/news/2021/04/06/lgbt-students-sue-education-department-over-title-ix-religious-exemption

Reese, W. J. (2005). *America's public schools: From the common school to 'no child left behind'*. The Johns Hopkins University Press.

Sanchez, M. (2019). *Queer faith: Reading promiscuity and race in the secular love tradition*. NYU Press.

Schulman, S. (2016). *Conflict is not abuse: Overstating harm, community responsibility, and the duty of repair*. Arsenal Pulp.

CHAPTER 1

Reorienting Conversations On Religious And Queer Discourses

IN OCTOBER 2020, sixth-grade history teacher Steve Arauz was fired from Lake Forest Education Center, a Seventh-Day Adventist school in Florida. He was fired for being gay (Maxwell, 2020). A year prior, as Maxwell reported, a theater teacher, Monica Toro Lisciandro, was fired from Covenant Christian School, also in Florida. She was fired for having a girlfriend. In both cases, these teachers were fired for being gay or lesbian by religiously affiliated schools that received public funding through Florida's various voucher/tax credit programs. Reporting for the *Orlando Sentinel*, Maxwell noted that alongside these two firings, "dozens of publicly funded voucher schools in Florida blatantly discriminate against LGBTQ students and families" (2020, para. 7). Although after the reporting many of these schools scrubbed their websites of such explicit discrimination, the discrimination itself persisted, showing that "children are being taught to discriminate. With tax dollars" (para. 12). Such discrimination, Maxwell, continued, "is defended by the governor, education commissioner, legislative leaders and even the leading nonprofit that administers the state's voucher program" (para. 13). Such discrimination, as well, was not only directed against teachers but also students and their families.

The issues raised in Florida are not unique to Florida as cases of LGBTQ+ teachers being fired for being gay are not new, nor is the discrimination against LGBTQ+ students and their families. Rather, such firings have been documented recently, for instance, in Indiana and Ohio (Riley, 2020), Texas (Platoff, 2018), and Washington state (Madani, 2020). Each of these cases involves a religiously affiliated school with the firings rooted in "religious freedom" arguments that manifest in exemptions from antidiscrimination policies (e.g., Title IX). These arguments came to the fore particularly under the Trump administration, although they have a much longer history within ideological struggles around public education as it inevitably intersects with religion.

Religious expression butts up against sexual (and gender) expression in these cases in a continued pitched battle amidst the ongoing work of democracy and public education. The history of American public education is, as various historians and commentators have documented, intimately tied to religion (e.g., DelFattore, 2004; Labaree, 2010; Reese, 2005). These intimate ties are complex, and they document the continued conflict and contestations that have emerged at various moments in U.S. history. This is a theme taken up by Burke and Segall (2017) in an attempt to surface the many ways in which the commonsense of education in the United States is rooted in Christian understandings of student possibility, linguistic choices, and metaphors (see also Blumenfeld et al., 2008).

Such conflicts and contestations make sense on the surface given the history of the United States not only as a nation founded on particular ideas of religious freedom but also as a nation whose demographics have shifted massively over time, making visible religious pluralism. While Christians, as the Pew Research Center's Religious Landscape Study (2015) documented, make up approximately 70.6% of the U.S. population, no particular sect of Christianity enjoys close to that number in relative terms. Evangelical Protestants make up 25.4% of the population; Catholics, 20.8%; and Mainline Protestants, 14.7%. Historically Black Protestant denominations comprise 6.5%, Mormons claim 1.6%, and other Christian sects clock in with under 1%. Non-Christian faiths, including Jews (1.9%), Muslims (0.9%), Hindus (0.7%), and Buddhists (0.7%), account for 5.9% of the population. Additionally, a total of 22.8% of the population are unaffiliated or what Pew labels as "religious 'nones.'" Alongside these demographic numbers, Gallup showed that in 2021, fewer than half of U.S. adults (47%) belonged to a church, synagogue, or mosque, the first time the number has been below 50% in the eight decades of Gallup's poll (Jones, 2021). We can see simply looking at the religious landscape of the United States, captured by Pew and Gallup (2015), that religion is something that cannot be ignored—even as it perhaps recedes in importance—as it presents a variety of challenges and, we hope, opportunities for thinking about and within public education.

Just as with religion, gender and sexuality have, in a different way, always been present and contested in American public education's histories. For instance, Catherine Beecher's advocacy in the mid-19th century for women as teachers, as Nancy Hoffman documented (1981), provided women an opportunity to work and extend the domestic sphere. This helped bring women (primarily White middle-class women) into the workforce and codify the feminization of teaching, legacies still with us on both accounts. There is, of course, extensive literature on the ways in which schools shape gender possibility and performance alongside sexuality and race (e.g., Ferguson, 2001; Kehler & Atkinson, 2010; Pascoe, 2007; Thorne, 1993). Vanessa Siddle Walker in *The Lost Education of Horace Tate* (2018) uncovered the legacies of race as they intersected with gender and religion to tell the stories of countless Black educators who worked tirelessly to establish just teaching and learning conditions for Black children. Concerns about women's role in teaching evolved throughout the 19th and 20th centuries, as documented by Jackie Blount in *Fit to Teach* (2005). Blount's historical analysis illustrates the ways in which gender and same-sex desires, while arguably present throughout the history of American public schooling, have taken on different meanings and controversies through the years. These meanings and controversies have changed over time both due to politics (e.g., Women's Liberation, Gay Liberation) and demographics. Women, as has been documented, account for slightly more than 50% of the American population with less stable demographic data available for LGBTQ+ individuals. The Williams Institute (2020), out of the University of California, Los Angeles, puts the number of LGBTQ+ individuals in the United States at about 4.5%. While a Gallup poll released in 2021 found a significant increase to 5.6% of Americans identifying as LGBT since its previous poll in 2017 when 4.5% identified as such (Morales, 2021). As is the case with demographics, the numbers get further nuanced as intersections are taken into account, adding further layers to these histories.

And so we see here, in a rather superficial manner, a complexity that has always been in play within American public education, which was founded amid a particular set of politics and a historically specific—read White, read male, read propertied—demographic. And within the democratic struggle, those politics and demographics have shifted in ways that have expanded access and inclusion fitfully certainly but nearly comprehensively as access to schooling expanded over the years to include previously disenfranchised populations (Anderson, 1988; Lugg, 2016; Spring, 2000; Valenzuela, 1999). This democratic struggle, of course, has never accomplished its task of full democratic participation in its entirety but, rather, continues to evolve in the face of changing politics and demographics. This evolution requires a certain critical hope. "Education, like democracy," as Michael Roth (2019) argues, "depends on hope—on a belief that we can find ways to improve our lives in common as well as our own individual lives" (p. 111).

The reality of public education as part of the founding as well as the evolution of American democracy ensures that students and teachers in public schools are a vital component of the commons. They are, thus, always buffeted by debates and contests with other stakeholders, among them parents and local communities. These debates and contests are multilayered as they address a range of issues, and these issues can be broken down to include for instance purpose, curriculum, and preparation.

There has never been, as David Labaree (2010) argues, a singular purpose for American public schools. Rather, throughout the history of public schools, there have existed, in grating proximity, a range of competing purposes. The competing purposes of American public schools, as he articulated, include democratic equality (cultivating citizens), economic efficiency (preparing individuals for the workforce), and social mobility (meritocracy). In addition to Labaree's delineation of these purposes, Gert Biesta (2005) added the purpose of developing unique subjects: bringing students into presence. This emphasis on education's role in subjectification added (or perhaps merely reemphasized) a philosophical purpose alongside the political and economic purposes elucidated by Labaree. These purposes, as Labaree argued, are competing and therefore often at odds with one another. It is, for instance, nigh on impossible to privilege economic efficiency while also seeking social mobility. And democratic equality is complicated by a focus on social mobility, which is rooted in creating different economic outcomes and therefore economic inequalities. We would add a fifth purpose, obvious enough for those emerging from backgrounds in curriculum theory: the socialization and normalization of a population. Here we find the ways in which schools utilize the hidden and/or null curricula to produce certain kinds of docile (or active) bodies most especially in relation to sexuality and gender presentation. This last purpose, in the American context, although not only in the American context, is run through with religious sensibilities, limitations, and violence. For indeed, another underlying purpose of public education, for a great many stakeholders in America, remains religious.

Alongside these competing purposes, which wax and wane in their relative importance and influence, there are histories of debates about the curriculum in schools and what students are meant to learn. Some of these take on metaphorical grandiose militaristic proportions as seen in the Math, Science, and Readings Wars of the 20th century; others take on histories of oppression, as seen in social justice advocacy and movements in multiculturalism, culturally relevant, sustaining, decolonial, and antiracist work. Such debates are themselves tied to what one takes to be the purpose of public education. Should the curriculum focus on skills and practical ideas that prepare students for particular jobs, or should the curriculum focus on big ideas and critical thinking to assist students in becoming reasonable citizens? Does the curriculum have a responsibility to right the wrongs of yesteryear or should the curriculum maintain some semblance of conserving a "great past"?

Our suspicions (and interests) are that such debates are provocative on the rhetorical level, allowing diverse parties and political persuasions to get in their say and be part of a democratic process. However, such debates at the rhetorical level played out in op-eds, political speeches, and research (be it labeled "activist" or otherwise) do not account for or dig into the complexities of bringing such diverse and competing views into classrooms, in conversations with and between students and teachers. Classrooms, those spaces where students and teachers meet, are complex environments that bring together diverse bodies, experiences, and ideas even within what might on a surface level look like a rather homogenous context. This intense interpersonal level, where educational relations are cultivated (or aren't), is implicated in the rhetorical level, where big ideas and arguments are debated, but the rhetorical level cannot fully account for the immense diversity that exists when the idea of "American Public Schooling" is broken down into its empirical realities, realities that document the successes and failures of a vast, complicated system.

The realities of American public schools are such that on any given day approximately one sixth of the U.S. population is directly involved as students, teachers, or staff. This one sixth of the population is then broken down into 50 different states, the District of Columbia, and across various U.S. territories, each with their own legal mandates and conceptualizations of public education, which are further delineated into districts, individual schools, and, finally, classrooms. These layers of difference become more and more complicated the more specific they become. For our purposes here, we focus specifically on U.S. contexts. We do this to recognize how histories and discourses often take on local flavors that can translate to other locales, which would require experiences and insights that our own subject positions do not provide. And yet, of course, "U.S. contexts" contain multitudes. Education researchers have themselves documented specific locales, be that, for instance, New Jersey (Anyon, 1981, 1997), Chicago (Ewing, 2018; Todd-Breland, 2018), or Los Angeles (Jaramillo, 2012). Each context provides a complex history and set of circumstances to think through common dreams and their failures within public schools. Combined, such local studies provide insights into the broader U.S. context, showing concretely how public schools are not only subjected to federal oversight but are also rooted in specific communities' challenges and practices. While we do not dig into specific locations, except for anecdotal purposes, we hope readers will find ways to think through their own contexts and positions to engage the knot of issues we explore around public education, religion, sexuality, and gender.

Labaree (2010) argues, in reference to the failures of school reform, that these decentralized complexities have been key in protecting American public schools from the successful implementation of various school reforms. Legal cases, which we explore in a later chapter, emerge themselves out of local school contexts, revealing the ongoing tensions and relations between local and federal control. These decentralized complexities also illuminate the possibilities and needs for continued engagement with teacher education and the ways it emerges in very different contexts and communities. Indeed, teacher education provides a space for students-becoming-teachers to both recognize the educational and school realities that not only helped form them but also allowed (or didn't allow) them to become mindful of the uncertainties and potentials contained within the complexities of American public schools. Issues around students becoming teachers and their struggles for identity are taken up in a later chapter, as well. While rhetorically we may talk about "the system," upon further reflection, we would do well to recognize the system is far more complex as we get closer to the ground. Or, put differently, we could read ourselves as mere cogs in the larger machinery of an industrial metaphor or contemplate the ways our digital world creates spaces where we might see glitches or become glitches that do different kinds of work (Russell, 2020). This is vital, we think, to engage within teacher education such that student teachers become cognizant of the importance of context and community while remaining mindful of the interconnectedness across educational situations amid changed discourses, metaphors, and technological revolutions.

For any educational scholar, choices have to be made about what realities to address, explore, and thus read. The beauty, we suggest, of educational research is that its immense diversity allows for the complexity of the so-called system to be addressed in different ways. The challenge of educational research is finding ways to utilize it to address, on the ground, the issues that such research illuminates. How do we thread in the lessons and findings of education research—as it emerges at levels of, for instance, history or society or culture—to engage student teachers within teacher education so that they are both informed by such research and mindful of the limits of it as it encounters the fleshy subjects of school? There is, after all, a danger when research is applied to different contexts or times as it can perpetuate harm or rely on simplified understandings that have shifted since the time of such research.

This question about the use and limits of education research applies to an array of issues taken up by educational scholars. Education research is implicated in any given historical moment as to what is considered viable research. Current demands for research that is practical is itself a demand with a history, as Popkewitz (2020) illustrated. Similarly, demands by student teachers for practical lessons, often with an explicit disdain for theory and research, reifies ideas that teaching is easy or can simply be prescribed. We do not want to reproduce arguments that pit theory against practice or forms of research against one another but will step to the side of such concerns to recognize the different work involved in teacher education that seeks to bring abstract commitments into concrete practices such that concrete practices help (in)form our abstract commitments. Neither, we suggest, can exist alone.

For our purposes, we engage in what can broadly be called "humanities-oriented research" to explore the complex intersections that exist when "religion," "sexuality," and gender" meet. A humanities-oriented approach to research, as explained by the American Educational Research Association (2009), seeks to "problematize unrecognized assumptions, implications, and consequences of various kinds of educational practice" (p. 482). There is a range of practices that we will look at in the coming pages in order to think through, and think anew about, the relationships between "religion," "sexuality," and "gender" as they have impacted and will continue to impact educational practices and lives. For instance, later in the book, we turn to contemplate the work of forgiveness and its paradoxes when thinking through harms as they exist when the intersections of religion, sexuality, and gender are engaged seriously in classrooms. Forgiveness is neither a given, nor required, but may prove generative as a practice to think with when navigating these issues and conflicts. For Koppelman (2020), we recognize that "no negotiation is thinkable, on any of these issues, if each side regards any deal as a betrayal of its deepest commitments" (p. 12). Forgiveness, we will suggest, may provide an opening volley in making things thinkable without the need to betray religious or queer-activist stances.

Central to this work is attending to the interplay of political, legal, moral, theological, and pedagogical discourses as they interact and manifest themselves in and through the identities of students, teachers, and student teachers. This interplay of discourses and embodied subjects is complex and inflected with controversies. We will inevitably touch on these controversies—this chapter opened with several of them—but we will also, we hope, find ways to engage these intersections hospitably. It is one of our beginning beliefs that may or may not bear out that religion, sexuality, and gender as matters of concern in education have more potential in continuing the hopes of democracy than mere antagonism, an orientation that has defined their interplay in research and the court of public opinion more often than not over the last half a century. This is made visible with the emergence of the modern conservative movement, gay liberation, the realization of LGBTQ+ rights, and the conflicts of such rights with religious freedom.

To find these common grounds, however, we sense there is a need for conversations that do justice to and build on the ideas and concepts rooted in religious, sexual, and gendered experiences. After all, it remains the case that students and teachers bring into classrooms complex identities that include their religious, sexual, and gender identities. Each of these, while at times analytically distinct, cannot be distinguished on an embodied level because they exist within one's (conception of) self. There is conflict here given the ways in which religion, sexuality, and gender are themselves pitted against one another in other ways. The work of becoming a self, of claiming identities, is impacted by these issues as they play out in our individual lives in relation to various institutions, including schools, family, and houses of worship. And it ought to be clear that although one might not attend a particular church, that does not limit the extent to which religion often inflects on individual and collective experiences in American education.

Within teacher education—which is the part of the broader field of education in which we situate ourselves—the work of becoming a teacher has to grapple with the interplay of religion as it is brought to bear on gendered and sexual experiences both because teachers are embodied and because the ways teacher education does or does not engage such embodiment impacts the experiences of students coming into presence themselves. We want to not only set the stage in this chapter for our work but also provide you, our readers, with our understanding of some broad categories that we see as central to our explorations. These include teacher education, curriculum studies, and the work of conversation. And each of these areas emerges from complex heritages and debates. We offer the following not as an exhaustive overview but as a specific engagement with how we have been informed by particular instantiations of those areas of inquiry and practice. We hope doing so allows you to join us in this conversation, take the conversation in different directions in your own time and place, and continue these conversations as they evolve and change.

We are, ourselves, inspired by rhetorician Kenneth Burke's (1941) rather well-worn parlor metaphor of unending conversation and its complications. Burke wrote:

> Imagine that you enter a parlor. You come late. When you arrive, others have long preceded you, and they are engaged in a heated discussion, a discussion too heated for them to pause and tell you exactly what it is about. In fact, the discussion had already begun long before any of them got there, so that no one present is qualified to retrace for you all the steps that had gone before. You listen for a while, until you decide that you have caught the tenor of the argument; then you put in your oar. Someone answers; you answer him; another comes to your defense; another aligns himself against you, to either the embarrassment or gratification of your opponent, depending upon the quality of your ally's assistance. However, the discussion is interminable. The hour grows late, you must depart. And you do depart, with the discussion still vigorously in progress. (pp. 110–111)

Education scholars and practitioners are always in the midst of heated debates, and such debates have expanded to include more voices bringing different experiences and views to the table. We enter these debates in the late 2010s and the start of the 2020s amid intense polarization, struggles for racial justice, and a global health pandemic. While we, in some regards, hope to lower the temperature on some of these debates, such a lowering is not to displace the issues, but come at the issues differently. We think the existence of the debates themselves is central to the ongoing realization of democracy and difference does not require heightened temperatures. We recognize, as well, that engaging in such complicated conversations places different subjects in potentially difficult or awkward situations. No one enters conversations from a neutral place. This reality asks us to remember that in engaging in such conversations, we have to take seriously the ways in which the different positions and complex identities of student teachers and teacher educators come into play.

On Teacher Education

Hannah Arendt (1954/2006), in "The Crisis in Education," argues:

> Education is where we decide whether we love our children enough not to expel them from our world and leave them to their own devices, nor to strike from their hands the chance of undertaking something new, something unforeseen by us, but to prepare them in advance for the task of renewing a common world. (p. 193)

For Arendt, a perennial task for teachers is, among other things, finding a balance within the intergenerational dynamic that is ever present in education. This is the work of love. How do teachers bring students up in the world in which they were born so they won't flounder without supports while also not getting bogged down with that world's history such that they are unable to undertake something new? This intergenerational dynamic of balancing was for Arendt central to preparing students to become part of the work of "renewing a common world." Yet, as we have unpacked in prior work (Burke & Greteman, 2013; Greteman & Burke, 2017) and explore later, love may not (or, rather, ought not) be the central decision in teacher education. Instead, it may be within the 21st century that teacher education is where we decide whether we like student teachers enough to both usher them into educational discourses and practices while holding space for their contributions to the work of cultural preservation and transformation.

Arendt's central concern was not the education of teachers—teacher education—whereby those students from schools begin to make a transition into the "adult" world to become teachers themselves. This generational flip amid the ongoing renewal of a common world illustrates that such work is never complete but forever ongoing. Student teachers encounter within teacher education another intergenerational dynamic, one in which they are caught in the proverbial middle. They are the incoming "adults" to schools wrestling with how to distinguish themselves from the students they now teach (but are often only removed from by a few short years). Yet they are also still students now tasked with thinking about education differently, most particularly how they will enter into educational relations that are no longer defined by their position as a student responsible for their own education, but as a teacher responsible for the education of, as Lisa Delpit (2006) poignantly argues, "other people's children."

It is this dynamic in which positions of "student and teacher" along with "child and adult" are in flux that complicates the everyday work of teacher education. As teacher educators ourselves, we want to ground our own approach in this dynamic to recognize the ways in which the work of educating teachers is also a place where "we have to decide." Our decision, for some, might be viewed as once removed from the children of preK–12 schools, but we suggest that it is intimately related to these schools when looked at through a multigenerational lens. Elementary schools feed secondary schools, which feed colleges, universities, and trade schools as students progress toward adulthood, and amid such a progression, teacher education students return to elementary and secondary schools as teachers. The work of education—at any level—is never atomistic (a point well made by Nespor, 1997, in spatial terms), making it necessary to contemplate how the work in any one area impacts another area and vice versa. Teacher education, as a field, is but one component of this reality. It is a field dotted with diverse programs that take up different views on the purpose(s) of education and what it takes to become a good teacher. It is, as well, quite often in the crosshairs of politics. We recognize these complex histories and politics while wanting to dig into and explore a specific set of issues that are either treated separately or completely ignored.

Throughout this book, we are invested in exploring the tensions and potentials at intersections that are present when "religion," "sexuality," and "gender" discourses and identities enter the teacher education classroom. Our exploration, we hope, can be extended into more general classrooms in higher education where such issues exist as well without the added layer implicated in teacher education. We focus on teacher education specifically and what we consider to be its somewhat unique classroom, which is simultaneously preparing students to become teachers themselves by thinking about and through instructional, curricular, and pedagogical strategies while also providing those same students with an education themselves in the histories, philosophies, theories, and practices of education, not to mention, of course, the specific insights rooted in the different subject areas (e.g., social studies, art, English, science, physical education). This dynamic, in the everydayness of teaching, offers teacher educators an opportunity to think with students not only about how they might teach their future students, but about the very encounter of education they, as "student teachers," are amid. Teacher education, in other words, exists at this complex intersection of a "professional" program focused on educating future professionals alongside a "liberal" education that, as Michael S. Roth (2019) argues, "should inspire civic participation in ways that allow students to connect with people who share their views and to engage with those who don't" (p. 110). In addition to these internal purposes, teacher education also has a responsibility for engaging local communities that support and condition how student teachers gain experience in "apprentice" or "student teaching" experiences. Teacher education programs are never only situated in the so-called ivory tower but are intimately connected to the local (and sometimes so local) contexts in which their students' student-teach. What should we say, for instance, when students approach our student teachers and let them know they will be praying for them? What should we do when our own student teachers do the same for us, especially when they imply that they are praying for our conversion? Is our job to "convert" them into something different, someone who does not wish to convert us?

For Guilfoyle et al. (1995), this requires thinking as well about professors of teacher education who, as they note, "must negotiate multiple layers of institutional politics and policies, both in the teaching of teachers and in the participation and negotiation necessary to continue with the academy" (p. 37). Amid such negotiations, there is a reminder that "teaching is always a political activity" and that "politics can be even more difficult in teacher education because of its lower status within the university and the larger culture and the increased number of institutional connections that educating teachers demands" (p. 37). These on-the-ground realities have dramatically shifted since the mid-1990s after multiple economic recessions and turns to austerity that have impacted school budgets and personnel in different ways depending on context. Common across contexts, however, are the tensions that become part of the educational encounter. Negotiating the politics and economic realities within a university, within a school district, and within individual schools requires deft handling of contentious issues not only as they operate in the curriculum but also within the embodied experiences of students, teachers, and student teachers. But the larger point is that in the United States, politics is also religious. And so failing to think with and about (rather than necessarily against) the religious elements that drive the politics of education and teacher education means missing trees, adorned with crosses, for the forest in which they grow. We don't need to necessarily rip the crosses off the trees, and we certainly don't want to burn the forest down, so what best ought we do?

Student teachers can, in teacher education, of course, seek to avoid their own education and its necessary discomforts in favor of learning how to teach, which, through their years of "apprenticeship of observation" (Lortie, 1975), they may think is rather easy. Yet learning to teach, much like teaching, is not easy. Rather, it involves at least partially unlearning one's own assumptions and ideas about teaching alongside navigating the complex terrain of teaching and learning. This tension arises for professors of teacher education who, themselves, are navigating similar politics and demands while working to teach their own student teachers.

On the first count addressing the learning of student teachers, Deborah Britzman (2007) reminds us that unlearning involves countering the avalanche of experience from our own schooling. Within teacher education, she argues,

> our opening problem is this: we have grown up in schools, have
> spent our childhood and adolescence observing teachers and our
> peers. . . . Growing up in education permeates our meanings of

> education and learning; it lends commotion to our anticipations
> for and judgements toward the self and our relations with others.
> It makes us suspicious of what we have not experienced and lends
> nostalgia to what has been missed. Simply put, our sense of self and
> our sense of the world is profoundly affected by having to grow up
> in school. (p. 2)

We grow up in school, carry lessons forward with us, but also encounter the failures of such lessons. For teacher educators, the reality is that our students, upon graduation, become the individuals teaching in their own classrooms and, thus, face many of the same intersections and tensions they faced as "students" but from the other side of the student–teacher hyphen.

These tensive intersections have, over the past few years, become perhaps more salient due to the larger political realities ushered in, in part, by the presidency of Donald Trump. We cannot give Trump all the credit for the heightened partisanship, which built on previous political machinations, but we would do well to recognize that the heightened partisanship and polarization made apparent during his presidency will last long after his last day in office, including policies around deregulation and continued assaults on teacher certification requirements. For Michael Roth (2019), however, "partisanship may be a fact of life in politics these days, but the presence on campus of different diversities shows that education need not succumb to it" (p. 123). Here we do not want to succumb to the ways religion, sexuality, and gender discourses are often pitted against one another, nor do we eschew our belief in the necessity of teacher education. Rather, drawing on David Labaree (2010), we recognize the complexities of teaching and teacher education such that,

> we ask teacher education programs to provide ordinary college
> students with the imponderable so that they can teach the ir-
> repressible in a manner that pleases the irreconcilable, and all
> without knowing clearly either the purposes or the consequences
> of their actions. (p. 231)

Continuing along the lines of these complexities, he adds,

> But that is not the end of the problem confronting teacher educa-
> tors. In addition, they face a situation in which the profession of
> teaching is generally seen to be relatively easy. And this perception
> is not simply characteristic of the untutored public; it is also en-
> demic among teacher candidates. (Labaree, 2010, p. 231)

So we enter this conversation together realizing that teacher education is not a monolith. Given the reality that ideologically, structurally, and peda-gogically diverse programs exist and take up different views on the purpose of education, the issues we explore will need to be revised and refracted through different contexts and communities. Yet, amid such diverse programs, there remains the perennial challenge of bringing students into the complicated conversations and practices of education in contexts and communities. Of par-ticular interest to our work in this book is the complicated conversation that emerges around "religion," "sexualities," and "genders," conversations that are never monolithic but tinged by the local flavors. Each of these broad concepts, as well, has an intricate past in education, implicating the material realities of not only student teachers but also teacher educators and preK–12 students. Still, while the past is implicated in our present, we cannot allow that past to dictate how we engage the conversations moving forward.

On Curriculum

In *Curriculum Studies in the United States: Present Circumstances, Intellec-tual Histories* (2013), William Pinar articulates the play between histories and presents as central to the work of curriculum. Pinar was angry about the present circumstances—notably the impact of billionaire philanthropists on educa-tion—but he was not without hope. Hope for Pinar came in thinking through the method he offered in conceptualizing (or reconceptualizing) "curriculum." And this method emerged through the concepts of "verticality" and "hori-zontality." These spatial terms ask us, via Pinar, to think across the terrain we presently experience while also gaining a deep understanding of our intellec-tual histories. Neither project is any good on its own—if we only pay attention to the present circumstances, then we miss out on how such circumstances came to be along with ways we might challenge such circumstances by using concepts from the past. Yet, if we only keep our attention on our "history," we stumble in the present since we are looking backward. So we need to—at different points—look around us at our present circumstances and investigate them seriously with an eye towards histories. This can be a challenge—we are made to recognize our own implications in the world and how that world has un/knowingly shaped us and, in that investigation, turn to both our personal and our intellectual histories that orient us to particular ways of understanding, thinking about, and being in the world.

Amid such work, Pinar (2013) asserts, "we are called to concepts through changing circumstances" (p. 69). The concepts we utilize every day are concepts that did not emerge naturally (as if such a thing as naturally even existed), but out of a unique mix of circumstances, responses to those circumstances, and a constellation of other realities (e.g., the politics of publishing, access to education). Yet we are not forced to merely reproduce these concepts but build on them in new, creative ways. For Pinar's purposes, our attention might fall to the banality of several concepts—power, resistance, reproduction—that once were quite critical and cutting edge. Now, however, they have become the taken-for-granted concepts that we can use without "thinking." They have become part of the background of curriculum theory, but we also would suggest teacher education more generally. Schools are reproductive (no, really, do we have to keep saying this). Students resist in all kinds of ways (well, of course, they do), and power is everywhere (wow, that's insightful, Captain Obvious).

Noting these realities, snarky as the approach may be, is not to discount such concepts and the important work they have done but to suggest the need to do something else with those concepts as they have changed and continue to change the landscapes of education, particularly teacher education. After all, the field of education has its own contested history, and it continues to face challenges to its purposes and existence. Teacher education's curriculum, itself, asks that we engage student teachers in complicated conversations that are not merely about technique and behavioral management but about the larger historical, philosophical, and theoretical issues in play alongside our present concerns, as well.

Our circumstances at the start of a new decade have changed in various ways from the emerging impact of Donald Trump's former presidency to the twinned pandemics of 1619 and 2019 (see Hannah-Jones, 2019). Within these circumstances, we want to converse our way through to new concepts that may provide ways to not only "think" about these circumstances but also teach within them in better ways. Amid diverse teacher education programs there remains the perennial challenge of bringing student teachers into the array of complicated conversations and practices of education that help them become part of schools as not only teachers (often romanticized) but also workers (with labor issues) and citizens (with political power). Central to our understanding of curriculum and teacher education, however, is a concern with how student teachers as they become teachers assist in bringing students, their future students, into their subjectness.

Liking in Education

Before teachers' eyes and ears, students are always in the midst of becoming subjects who, in time, articulate and position themselves within discourses through various practices. To think about sexuality, gender, and religion in education is to enter a thicket of conundrums, challenges, and possibilities in this process. Each of the concepts—sexuality, gender, and religion—is not singular and brings with it a whole range of issues that can expand and constrict education across time and place. These issues, from our personal embodiments as subjects, to their complicated historical and present-day circumstances, swirl about visibly and invisibly in the work of education. As teacher educators, our thinking is rooted in understanding education as a relational enterprise. And a question that guides our work is centered on liking the other. Liking the other, as we will unpack throughout this book, always already implicates the self. To like the other implicates the self who likes. As we encounter others in education, across and within generations, we are tasked with navigating diverse views and understandings of the imbrications of gender, sexuality, and religion. Loving and hating the other are, on the surface, probably more commonplace. There are tomes written on each of them, not to mention songs and films rooted in telling the stories of such intertwined concepts and feelings. Yet we want to contemplate the potential of a softer form of relating, arguably a bit mundane even, rooted in liking that brings us down to earth from the seemingly more divinely inspired love and hate.

Throughout this book, we offer a series of conversations that operate at the intersection of discourses around religion, gender, and sexuality. In engaging in this series of conversations, we attempt to avoid the extreme edges where love and hate rear their head, to sit instead in a less extreme state of liking (and perhaps disliking). Such conversations attempt to exchange ideas rooted in these discourses often marked as, in various ways, unwelcome in both public and private educational spaces. Specifically, we enter such conversations with particular emphasis in—often but not exclusively—Catholic theologies alongside queer theories. In engaging thusly across and within these discursive spaces—often rendered separately or in opposition to each other—we seek to think about and through the ways these discourses while steeped in discontent, dilemma, and difficulty might also offer opportunities to reorient ourselves amid 21st-century educational realities.

More to the point, the text puts queer histories and logics into conversations with theologies both approached in the vein of Ahmed's (2006) notion of a "queer genealogy." Such work, in the mixing of discourses often considered to be running on parallel lines or at loggerheads in their perpendicularity (raging against one another, in ways long understood), might "open up new kinds of connection" through their "coming into contact" again in new ways (p. 155). Such contact, we suspect, affects, in effect, new lines, oblique ones even onto which we might graft different thinking. Eschewing the typical antagonism that often defines the relationships between religious and queer discourses, this book engages resonances and overlaps that might provide new habits for conducting the work of meeting in educational worlds.

We take, then, as a guiding metaphor the notion of orientation in our work in teacher education. This, of course, plays on long-standing tropes about sexual orientation, a site of major contention and much violence both symbolic and material within, between, and among queer and religious discourses. Particularly, however, orientation takes up the challenge from Ahmed that we consider "how 'what' we think 'from' is an orientation device" (2006, p. 4), pointing us in certain future directions (and not others) while emerging from particularized histories (and not others). What we think from, then, in this text are queer and theological sources—in some cases, as well, queer theological ones. We will, at times, likely frustrate readers possessed of greater fluency in religious discourses with our conflation of the religious with the theological just as we will frustrate readers ensconced in queer theory with our, at times, fluid, if not casual, running together of sexual and queer discourses and the texts that emerge from and constitute them. These frustrations, these tensions, we think, are productive, necessary, and likely unavoidable, and although our intent is not to be careless nor certainly callous in our work, we do intend, in this dialogic text, to think together in heterogeneous ways, through the scrim of our own histories and limitations. But in the direction of new and different possibilities both for queer studies and for religious reengagement and most of all teacher education.

It is our sense that the general treatment of religion, through queer studies in our fields—roughly teacher education where we overlap, but then English education and art education as the Venn diagram spreads apart—has been rooted in the hermeneutics of suspicion nearly exclusively (Sedgwick, 2003, p. 124). That is to say that much treatment of the religious, to say nothing of its concurrent theoretical undercarriage, theology, is characterized by suspicion begetting endless paranoid reads. These paranoid readings of religious intentionality in education, for instance, are not *wrong*, but they are limited as, of course, "paranoia knows some things well and other things poorly" (p. 130). Clearly the same can be said for reparative readings: They are no panacea and know well just as they, too, know poorly. Our point is not to replace one reading for another but, as we have in other spaces (e.g., Burke & Greteman, 2013; Greteman & Burke, 2017), to try to argue to the side of long-entrenched antagonisms, acknowledging the utility, indeed the ethics and the necessity, of those antagonisms. This is why we offer heterogeneous readings that recognize the multiple ways in which discourses interact and generate possibilities. We understand that, in large part, Cris Mayo (2006) was right when she argued that "any commingling of religion and liberalism has only been to the detriment of queer people and attempts to make the disagreements between the two seem less weighty only make current efforts to improve actual queer lives harder" (p. 428). Yet Mayo's insight emphasizes the past—the "has only been"—leaving room to work for an altered commingling for what "will have been." We have, as well, the benefit, the reader will notice, of not emerging in this case, from a liberal theoretical tradition:[1] Queer studies and the theology with which we engage both arise from different, although we think complementary in many ways, radical spaces. And although we hold room for the very real ways in which religion has been used as a bludgeon against queer life, indeed quite materially so (and still) we sense openings of possibility worth exploring. In fact, James Alison puts a finer point on this concern within the Catholic context, writing that,

> the experience of many gay people is that the Church in some way or another kills us. Typically in official discourse we are a they, dangerous people whose most notable characteristic is not a shared humanity, but a tendency to commit acts considered to be gravely objectively disordered. Typically our inclusion within the structures of church life comes at a very high price. (2001, p. 45)

And yet, the vital point for Alison (2001) is that "God has nothing to do with religious violence" (p. xiii). Religious violence is the creation of humans. It is not intrinsic (nor limited) to any given religious tradition and, as such, something that can be countered within and through religious logics. Some of this book is helping make sense of, holding space for, such assertions and their requisite critiques, in conversation both with one another as collaborators and with a range of scholars and their work.

In a volume that laid out the argument for humanizing approaches in qualitative research, Kinloch and San Pedro (2014) utilized Bakhtinian dialogicality to consider the value of listening as a project of research. Much of their argument was about the ways in which utterances of support (mmm-hmm; yep, I hear you, etc.) in the interstices of discussion serve as amplifiers—or perhaps scaffolds—for the speaker. They are ways in which listeners engage actively in supporting conversation partners, even amid disagreement. Because "ideological struggles result, in part, from listening with others as we consider, question, and debate diverse views that may, in fact, conflict with our own" (p. 27), the work of dialogicality, the authors argued is both about "openly listening to what is said and not said" (p. 28) as well as "allowing room for conflict, complications, silences, and pauses to exist between and among people as they learn to listen to each other *in the space between* language and silence, language and action" (p. 29). The structure of this text seeks to both engage the conflicts of the discourses it thinks with (roughly, religious ones and queer ones) while also creating a space for the silences and complications of two scholars, from similar yet very different backgrounds at the same time, to emerge and if not reconcile, at least form into conversation. The as-yet silent third partner in the discussion is, of course, the reader—the fourth we ought to acknowledge are the interlocutors on whom we draw through citational practice—and so welcome, we're glad you're here.

Our expectation is that, in the space between our writing and your reading, a great deal of conflict may arise; we ask your indulgence that you consider our ignorance at the finer points of some of our work's riskier edges comes not from a lack of goodwill but from the inherent limitations of a reader's life: We only know so much and, in many cases, so little. We find it useful in later chapters to suggest that the process of reconciliation, if perhaps stripped of its sacramentality, might be a useful way to beg your indulgence through the process. More on this as we go, but we don't seek forgiveness or absolution for our faults so much as your attempts to help us reconcile our thinking on these topics with your own.

Scholarly Positions

We, as collaborators in conversation, write from particular subject positions. These positions provide us with constrained vantage points rooted in our, at times shared and at other times different, educations. Our educations touch on our formal schooling experiences within Catholic schools for K–12 education, situated within a metropolitan city and a rural small midwestern town, alongside our university experiences with Jesuits and/or the Fathers of the Holy Cross, and our doctoral educations together in a public land-grant institution. Our educations continue in our own teaching (and learning) at a public land-grant institution in the Bible Belt and a private art school in a midwestern financial postindustrial financial hub. Each schooling context subjected us to particular educational frameworks and general ideological viewpoints that brought us into the world that we were simultaneously being asked to help remake/transform. We suspect, as should become clear throughout the following conversations, that these shared but different educational experiences contribute to many of our shared curiosities, discomforts, and commitments as not only scholars and educators but also citizens living in the world.

School is, of course, never our only mode of education. We encounter(ed) in our lives other forms of education amid the church, families, and public media cultures, each subjecting us to different, diverse, and often contradictory ideas and practices. We cannot fully uncover or remember all these educational experiences and encounters, only recognize the reality that we as the conversing subjects writing here, have been and continue to be subjected to various ideas, practices, indeed conceptual frameworks, and more. Such subjection is complex and contradictory, pleasurable and painful, rooted in the ways our own bodies, modes of identifying in the world (e.g., gay and straight), and being identified by the world (e.g., male, White, cisgender, upper middle class) and invariably allows us to think/see/live in the world and therefore limit us just as well. This reality is not unique to us. Any subject becomes such through encountering acts of subjection that impact one's formation as a subject.

As should also be evident or become evident moving ahead is that these conversations are not veiled "debates" between two opposed positions, a format of writing that, while useful, is not our purpose. We do not ask you, as readers, to "take sides," nor do we, as conversationalists, seek to win one or the other over to a side. There are benefits to such a point–counterpoint approach allowing sides to be drawn and clarity, perhaps, found in the process. But we will leave such an approach to others, like Corvino et al. (2017), who take up such a project debating religious liberty and discrimination situated primarily in the law. While the law is implicated in our work, we are interested in how complex intersections of religion and sexuality play out and inform the work that takes place in classrooms as students, teachers, and curriculum meet.

This is not, to be up front, to say that this is a project seeking belonging. Rather, it is rooted in the ever-present realities of nonbelonging that, we suspect, are exposed amid the debates often visible between "religion" and "sexuality," whereby those in one camp feel as if they don't belong within the other camp. Projects of inclusion based on the logics of belonging, we fear, remain ever tied to particularities that are never able to be fully included, in part, because particularities evolve and can within ideological camps become diametrically opposed. What is lost within drives for inclusion, as we will work through in conversation, are differences themselves. Difference, as such, is not something to be tolerated through mere inclusion, but as Audre Lorde (1984) argues, "difference must be . . . seen as a fund of necessary polarities between which our creativity can spark like a dialectic" (p. 111). Differences assist in learning and creating, but we have to engage their complexities and their conflicts in ways that allow such differences to remain different while creating anew.

We take the notion of creation seriously and tend to read it through the lens that Biesta (2014) has pulled from John Caputo, a theologian who has written extensively using Derrida. Biesta, in thinking about risk in education, returns through Caputo to the dual creation narratives in the book of Genesis, delineating the difference between the different narrators' accounts of how, in the Hebrew scriptures, the world came to be. In the Yahwist narrative, God creates "something out of nothing" (Caputo [as cited in Biesta 2014], p. 13); in the Elohist account, God "is not responsible for the fact that elements are *there* but for the fact that they are fashioned and *called good*" (p. 14). This is the work of weak creation, which is to say not building new atoms but shaping them in ways that are deemed good. This is how we think of our work here: We are not building from nothing but putting different forms into conversation in search of a unique kind of good in teacher education that might allow us to do things differently together.

Our work here joins a range of conversations, notably those in teacher education and curriculum studies, that will continue after we are done amid changed conditions from those we write from. Throughout the remainder of this book, you will encounter a range of issues, ideas, conundrums that play out, in our estimation, in classrooms both at the preK–12 level and in teacher education, as religion, sexuality, and gender meet. Such meetings are never settled ahead of time, nor are they ever solely focused on themselves as they are joined by conversations of economics, race, ability, and so much more. We cannot, to state the obvious, consider everything here, although we will write about consideration later. We consider some things that we find relevant or interesting to our moment but offer them hesitantly so not to dominate the conversation. After all, the conversations we are joining have been going on for a long time, and these conversations will continue long after we are gone. We hope that in threading these conversations together that others might join such conversations in different ways to further contemplate the work of liking the other to get us to relate to not only these concepts differently but to one another as well.

Endnotes

1 Careful readers may balk at this assertion given the longer tail of a liberal tradition that is linked to Enlightenment ideals supposedly constructed in contrast to religious limitation and superstition. We acknowledge, of course, that fields of study in the academy on which we draw are indebted to this long-established

liberal tradition. We also understand notions that, for instance, poststructural critique emerges in reference to structuralism, itself a hallmark of something like classical liberalism. Still, we think of our distinction here as a political one: To queer engages a different *logic* of human possibility that sees itself as both radical and in rupture with prior theoretical orientations.

References

Ahmed, S. (2006). *Queer phenomenology: Orientations, objects, others*. Duke University Press.

Alison, J. (2001). *Faith beyond resentment: Fragments Catholic and gay*. Crossroad Publishing Group.

American Educational Research Association. (2009). Standards for reporting on humanities-oriented research in AERA publications. *Educational Researcher, 38*(6), 481–486.

Anderson, J. D. (1988). *Education of Blacks in the South 1860–1935*. University of North Carolina Press.

Anyon, J. (1981). Social class and school knowledge. *Curriculum Inquiry, 11*(1), 3–42.

Anyon, J. (1997). *Ghetto schooling: A political economy of urban educational reform*. Teachers College Press.

Arendt, H. (2006). The crisis in education. In *Between Past and Future* (pp. 170–193). Penguin. (Original work published 1954).

Biesta, G. J. J. (2005). Against learning: Reclaiming a language for education in an age of learning. *Nordisk Pedagogik, 25*, 54–66.

Biesta, G. J. J. (2014). *The beautiful risk of education*. Paradigm.

Blount, J. (2005). *Fit to teach: Same-sex desire, gender, and school work in the twentieth century*. SUNY Press.

Blumenfeld, W. J., Joshi, K. Y., & Fairchild, E. E. (Eds.). (2008). *Investigating Christian privilege and religious oppression in the United States*. Sense Publishers.

Britzman, D. (2007). Teacher education as uneven development: Toward a psychology of uncertainty. *International Journal of Leadership in Education, 10*(1), 1-12.

Burke, K. (1941). *The philosophy of literary form*. University of California Press.

Burke, K. J., & Greteman, A. J. (2013). Toward a theory of liking. *Educational Theory, 63*(2), 151–170.

Burke, K. J., & Segall, A. (2017). *Christian privilege in U.S. education: Legacies and current issues*. Routledge.

Corvino, J., Anderson, R. T., & Girgis, S. (2017). *Debating religious liberty and discrimination*. Oxford University Press.

DelFattore, J. (2004). *The fourth r: Conflicts over religion in America's public schools*. Yale University Press.

Delpit, L. (2006). *Other people's children: Cultural conflict in the classroom.* The New Press.

Ewing, E. (2018). *Ghosts in the schoolyard: Racism and school closings on Chicago's South Side.* University of Chicago Press.

Ferguson, A. A. (2001). *Bad boys: Public schools in the making of Black masculinity.* University of Michigan Press.

Greteman, A. J., & Burke, K. J. (2017). *The pedagogies and politics of liking.* Routledge.

Guilfoyle, K., Hamilton, M. L., Pinnegar, S., & Placier, M. (1995). Becoming teachers of teachers: The paths of four beginners. In T. Russell & F. Korthagen (Eds.). *Teachers who teach teachers: Reflections on Teacher Education.* (pp. 35-55). The Falmer Press.

Hannah-Jones, N. (2019, August 14). The 1619 Project. *New York Times.* https://www.nytimes.com/interactive/2019/08/14/magazine/1619-america-slavery.html

Hoffman, N. (1981). *Women's true profession: Voices from the history of teaching.* Harvard Education Press.

Jaramillo, N. E. (2012). *Immigration and the challenge of education: A social drama analysis in South Central Los Angeles.* Palgrave Macmillan.

Jones, J. M. (2021, March 29). *U.S. church membership falls below majority for first time.* Gallup. https://news.gallup.com/poll/341963/church-membership-falls-below-majority-first-time.aspx

Kehler, M., & Atkinson, M. (Eds.). (2010). *Boys' bodies: Speaking the unspoken* (Vol. 46). Peter Lang.

Kinloch, V., & Pedro, T. S. (2014). The space between listening and storying: Foundations for projects in humanization. In D. Paris & M. T. Winn (Eds.), *Humanizing research: Decolonizing qualitative inquiry with youth and communities* (pp. 21–42). Sage Publications.

Koppelman, A. (2020). *Gay rights vs. religious liberty: The unnecessary conflict.* Oxford University Press.

Labaree, D. (2010). *Someone has to fail: The zero-sum game of public schooling.* Harvard University Press.

Lorde, A. (1984). *Sister outsider: Essays and speeches.* Ten Speed Press.

Lortie, D. C. (1975). *Schoolteacher.* University of Chicago Press.

Lugg, C. (2016). *U.S. Public schools and the politics of queer erasure.* Palgrave Macmillan.

Madani, D. (2020). *Seattle-area teachers reported fired for being gay; Catholic school says they resigned.* NBC News. https://www.nbcnews.com/feature/nbc-out/outcry-seattle-teachers-were-fired-being-gay-catholic-school-says-n1137546

Maxwell, S. (2020). Another gay teacher fired. LGBTQ students face expulsion. Discrimination in Florida schools. *Orlando Sentinel.* https://www.orlandosentinel.com/opinion/scott-maxwell-commentary/os-op-gay-teacher-fired-florida-scott-maxwell-20201023-mnfwdiqejrd2blf4cermulgeji-story.html

Mayo, C. (2006). Pushing the limits of liberalism: Queerness, children, and the future. *Educational Theory, 56*(4), 469-487.

Morales, C. (2021, February 24). More adult Americans are identifying as L.G.B.T., Gallup poll finds. *New York Times*. https://www.nytimes.com/2021/02/24/us/lgbt-identification-usa.html

Nespor, J. (1997). *Tangled up in school: Politics, space, bodies, and signs in the educational process* (J. Spring, Ed.). Lawrence Erlbaum.

Pascoe, C. J. (2007). *Dude, you're a fag: Masculinity and sexuality in high school*. University of California Press.

Pew Research Center. (2015, May 12). America's changing religious landscape. https://www.pewforum.org/2015/05/12/americas-changing-religious-landscape/

Pinar, W. (2013). *Curriculum studies in the United States: Present circumstances, intellectual histories*. Palgrave Macmillan.

Platoff, E. (2018). A gay Texas teacher is on leave after she showed students a photo of her wife. She has few legal protections. *Texas Tribune*. https://www.texastribune.org/2018/05/24/mansfield-isd-texas-art-teacher-LGBTQ-few-legal-protections/

Popkewitz, T. (2020). *The impracticality of practical research: A history of contemporary sciences of change that conserve*. University of Michigan Press.

Riley, J. (2020). Gay teacher fired from Dayton-area Catholic school after being outed to archbishop. *MetroWeekly*. https://www.metroweekly.com/2020/04/gay-teacher-fired-from-dayton-area-catholic-school-after-being-outed-to-archbishop

Roth, M. (2019). *Safe enough spaces: A pragmatist's approach to inclusion, free speech, and political correctness on college campuses*. Yale University Press.

Reese, W. J. (2005). *America's public schools: From the common school to "No Child Left Behind."* Johns Hopkins University Press.

Russell, L. (2020). *Glitch feminism: A manifesto*. Verso.

Sedgwick, E. (2003). *Touching feeling: Affect, pedagogy, performativity*. Duke University Press.

Spring, J. (2000). *Deculturalization and the struggle for equality: A brief history of the education of the dominated in the United States*. McGraw-Hill.

Thorne, B. (1993). *Gender play: Girls and boys in school*. Rutgers University Press.

Todd-Breland, E. (2018). *A political education: Black politics and education reform in Chicago since the 1960s*. University of North Carolina Press.

Valenzuela, A. (1999). *Subtractive schooling: U.S.–Mexican youth and the politics of caring*. SUNY Press.

Walker, V. S. (2018). *The lost education of Horace Tate*. The New Press.

Williams Institute. (2020). *LGBT data & demographics*. UCLA School of Law. https://williamsinstitute.law.ucla.edu/visualization/lgbt-stats/?topic=LGBT#density

CHAPTER 2

Liking The Other And Lowering The Temperature

A Preliminary Conversation

Kevin: We have this ongoing text message thread that's filled with ambivalent news about religion and queer issues. One or the other of us is attending—or has Google alerts set up—to the news with an eye toward our shared project. This isn't that unique amongst co-researchers, I don't think. But what we keep settling on is the idea that there's no panacea in the work of understanding the ongoing landscape of educational issues at the intersection of the intersubjective. We have student teachers who are members of the LGBTQ+ community who have experienced generativity in religious commitment just as we have student teachers who have, of necessity, left their faith in order to more fully embrace queer lives. There's a range of options in between there, and we don't ever want to undermine the very real ongoing uses of religion for hate. But we want to figure out what to do in our teacher education classrooms not only when that hate happens but also when something else happens too.

Adam: Some time ago, as a way into these issues, we found ourselves intrigued by and interested in the concept of "liking." This led to our first co-authored book *The Pedagogies and Politics of Liking* (Greteman & Burke, 2017), in which we really began the work of contemplating not only what "liking" is but also what it might do for us when thinking about education. This book continues to create a path for liking that, for me, wants to navigate the world to the side of more well-known, -worn, -felt, and -theorized concepts (and emotions) of love and hate. In this book, I hope we bring this thinking more directly into teacher education and how "liking," particularly the other, which also implicates the self, might assist us in navigating incredibly volatile and polarized times. This volatility and polarization are larger and more complicated than we can engage in one book, which is why we limit ourselves to thinking about "LGBTQ+" and "religious" issues. Both LGBTQ+ and religion are fraught in education, and this fraughtness is seen through the layers of education. They are topics to be considered in the classroom through the curriculum; they are embodied through student and teacher identities; they are discourses that contribute concepts to how we think and feel the world; they interact with one another historically. Each of these layers raises a host of concerns that various scholars and activists have sought to explore and/or advocate for in various ways. For me, our contribution, I hope, will be to assist individuals amid teacher education (both faculty and student teachers) to engage in conversations about these thorny and knotty problems to move past reproducing antagonisms that we might do something else.

Kevin: When I was in grade school, I was fortunate to have this really wonderful, stern, caring teacher named Mrs. Turner for both first and second grade. I'm not sure what was going on at Sutherland School at the time, but there must have been more freedom to make certain kinds of pedagogical choices in Chicago Public Schools in the mid-1980s than happens now because for those 2 years, the first- and second-grade classes were combined. I have a sense that Mrs. Turner, a longtime veteran, had a preference for the mixed-age format and convinced her colleagues across these grades that they, too, might try a bit of an experiment. In any event, what this meant was that we developed friendships that might not have otherwise been possible with kids who were a year older than us as first graders. It also put us in proximity to older students on whom, in short order, many of us developed really passionate early-career crushes.

Cut to a discussion with an older kid also named Kevin, whom a few of us were trying to get to admit to an undying love for a particular girl. Now the trick is, of course, that all of us in the group had a thing for her; this was pure projection. Kevin, however, the focal point at the time, tried to defuse a potentially explosive situation. He told us he "liked her from the bottom of [his] heart." Second-grade logic here, but he figured that the bottom of the heart meant she ranked really low on his list of priorities. Those of us schooled in the idioms of love, however, pounced on this incontrovertible evidence that he LIKED HER THE MOST ANYONE COULD EVER LIKE SOMEONE. I bring it up, this early miscommunication in the ways of the heart, to suggest that some of what we're trying to do here is flip the orientation of our emotional connections to—often as constructed dissonances from—others and ultimately the imagined other. The work here is about thinking about liking the other from the bottom of our hearts and replacing the supposed passion of that sort of statement with the indifference that Kevin tried to convey to us all those years ago in Mrs. Turner's class. We don't want to root our work in his confusion, in our misunderstanding his words, but rather, we want it linked to a sense that sometimes our notion of the gravity of a situation, as it connects to the humanity of others, might be diffused through a complacency of simply liking, from the bottom, top, or middle of the heart, with no commitment beyond this shared acknowledgment of humanity.

An Opening

There is a simple albeit politically tenuous need that grounds the conversations throughout this book. It is a need to metaphorically "lower the temperature." This is, arguably, a fraught thing to put to print given the ways in which different sides will claim their interlocutors are responsible for the mercury rising. In a polarized society, looking into the future can seem a peering out into an abyss of projection: What we hope will happen is often what we see off in the distance. Will the temperature continue to rise, reaching a boiling point, with animosity and hate overflowing? Will it rise but be tempered out through state interventions? Or will our better angels prevail, cooling off our heated selves, steam emitted in various forms without any real catastrophe occurring, but hopefully necessary changes taking hold? Oh, the metaphors we might extend! When looking into an abyss of the future, the possibilities while not endless are multitudinous, rooted inevitably in the decisions that are made across the spectrum—from our everyday decisions to the decisions of those in positions of power. Educators, particularly K–12 educators and teacher educators, are on the front lines of engaging students coming into these realities and developing ways of understanding, talking, and living amid and through such a time. Of course, educators are not the only ones responsible for taking on this work but exist alongside others who form and inform the way people live in the world.

One area, among many, where polarization is most visible is at the intersection of religion and LGBTQ rights. Prior to the 1970s, as shown by Putnam and Campbell (2010), religion cut across political ideologies. Religion within the broader history of the United States, as they illustrated, was rarely aligned with a particular political party but, instead, could be seen struggling alongside various political causes (e.g., abolition of slavery, advocacy for slavery, fights against sweatshops, arguments for the morality of work, civil rights marches and their denunciation from pulpits nationwide). It was, to put it differently, viable to be political and religious without one's political party tracking inevitably with any specific religious stance. Any number of political struggles noted earlier, as well as including things like the New Deal, would not have been possible without religion. Yet, starting in the 1970s, an alignment between religion and the conservative right emerged and calcified, which, decades later, has led to a consonant neglect of the religious left as it exists and in its political stances. This was something former president Barack Obama noted during the 2008 presidential election in the pages of *Christianity Today*. In a question-and-answer with Pulliam and Olsen (2008), Obama noted, "There's been a set of habits of thinking about the interaction between evangelicals and Democrats that we have to change" (para. 6). Continuing, he said, "Democrats haven't shown up. Evangelicals have come to believe oftentimes that Democrats are anti-faith" (para. 6). This habit of thinking has not changed, so much so that by the 2016 presidential election, Hillary Clinton did little to no campaigning for evangelical votes. When the dust settled on the 2016 election, she had received only 16% of the evangelical vote, the lowest of any Democratic presidential candidate, while her showing among Catholic voters was evenly split with Donald Trump (Blumberg, 2017). Noting this is not, to be clear, to place blame on Clinton's campaign, we, rather, mean it to illustrate the decades-long trend of Democrats (and, more generally, the left) of forgoing engagement with evangelicals and other religious voters. Instead, the left ceded religious discourses to the right (with, of course, exceptions), often painting religion, as such, with the broad brushstroke of intellectual vacuity and bigotry (Harris, 2005; Hitchens, 2007).

However, this move to cede religious discourses to the right and align the left with secular discourses failed to capture the large swath of a religious left, both historically and contemporarily. The narratives that arise out of these moves and alignments construct particular kinds of stories about conservative and progressive ideas about sexuality. Religion, never a monolith, is multitudinous as is secularism, with neither being aligned entirely along with progressive or conservative thought. We might, following Mary Lou Rasmussen (2016), grapple with relationships among secularisms to challenge the binary construction between the secular and the religious—the conservative and the progressive—particularly around sexualities. Indeed, the central organizing principle in the field of secularism over recent decades has been its shift to thinking in pluralities. Jakobsen and Pellegrini (2008) encapsulate this, noting that "the choice between secularism and religion represents a false dichotomy ... because religious and secular formations are profoundly intertwined with each other" (p. 11). Just as religion, conceptually, begets multiple and specific religious discourses as they arise from various practices, dogmas, and histories, so, too, then, do the attendant secularisms come to "vary with the religious formation in relation to which they develop" (p. 12). Secular formations, in the end, emerge in response to religious discourses and are thus colored by these discourses themselves. Certain critics (Heyes, in press) are clear, then, that there is no secularism that isn't inherently religious in its structure. Understanding this, we are freer to think about imbrication: What points of contact across supposed secular and religious divides allow for new ways of thinking about how to become in the world?

A part of our interest here is to engage these not-so-disparate realities to think through ways, drawing on Obama's earlier sentiment, to change habits of thinking. This includes drawing on the religious left and the ways they have sought to lower the temperatures often raised by the religious right. But it also means engaging the religious right and contemplating ways in which their viewpoints need to be considered within the broader democratic project. This presents a problem for contemporary democratic education. Yet, as Charles Taylor (2011) reminds us, "the problem is that a really diverse democracy can't revert to a civil religion, or anti-religion, however comforting this might be, without betraying its own principles" (p. 48). Such accommodations are fraught, so we limit our own attention to them within the classroom space as student teachers work to make sense of their own selves amid their emerging responsibilities as public educators. Such work is complicated and complex as student teachers begin the transition from students who may have particular protections and rights to teachers who become responsible, in new ways, for their own students and take on heightened scrutiny for their work as public employees.

We turn, in this chapter, to the work of "liking the other" as a way to begin conversations and lower the temperature. Our turn to liking the other follows not only our previous work grappling with these very tensions between religion and sexuality (Burke & Greteman, 2020) but also our broader project exploring the word like and the work of liking (Burke & Greteman, 2013). In our work *The Pedagogies and Politics of Liking* (Greteman & Burke, 2017), we followed the word *like* around to see what it does in different contexts (e.g., universities) and forms (e.g., popular, philosophical, theological). Of particular importance to our work here is the way Catholic theologian James Alison (2003) sought to tell a different theological story. In *On Being Liked*, he argues that "like" opens up in distinction from, in important ways, love, because,

> the word 'like,' is rather more difficult to twist into a lie than the word 'love', because we know when someone likes us. We can tell because they enjoy being with us, alongside us, want to share our time and company. (p. 107)

Continuing, Alison suggests:

> If our understanding of being loved does not include being liked, or at least being prepared to learn to be liked, then there's a good chance that we're talking about the sort of love that can slip a double bind over us, that is really saying to us "my love for you means that I will like you if you become someone else." (p. 107)

To like, in Alison's view, is to "be glad to be with us." Being with others, others one likes, asks that in liking the other, one "looks at us with the delight of one who enjoys our company, who wants to be one with us, to share in something with us" (Alison, 2003, p. 108). This feels, in many ways, similar to the ways in which we have come to understand our relationships with our students over the years: a fondness not weighted with the deep emotional ties and heavy ontological commitments that emerge from a compulsion to love. However, as Alison noted, love is not to be discarded. Rather, love, if it is to be taken seriously, needs to include liking.

Still, such a sentiment rooted in liking may sound a bit romantic, perhaps even naïve, amid our polarized times as, indeed, there are habits of mind out of which we would hope our students will eventually emerge. However, our turn to like aims to open up a different story to tell and therefore enact in our everyday as we encounter others: The work of teaching isn't about changing our students forcibly through the heavy application of love. It is about accompanying them in their work of becoming teachers where their failure to change isn't about our failure to teach but is, rather, about agential decisions emerging from complex conversations. Liking the other, we hope to illustrate not only in this chapter but throughout this book, is about the importance of drawing on concepts and stories that do different work. Or, as Donna Haraway (2016) has it, we recognize that "liking the other" might matter because,

> it matters what matters we use to think other matters with; it matters what stories we tell other stories with; it matters what knots knot knots, what thoughts think thoughts, what ties tie ties. It matters what stories make worlds, what worlds make stories. (p. 12)

Education, through its everyday relations between others, is implicated in both the making of stories and the telling of stories. Such stories not only reveal matters of concern but also illuminate what thoughts are privileged. They require, no matter what, our constant vigilance and creativity. Our move to liking the other is, we hope, not an answer to the range of questions we raise but a way to respond to the ethical work of education, work in which people within and across generations meet one another. It is, in many ways, another pebble thrown into the pond of ideas and practices to help shift relations in ways that grapple with and do justice to the complexities of becoming subjects through, in particular, schooling.

Habitual Thinking

The current habits of thinking started to calcify through the culture wars starting in the 1970s over the struggle around emerging rights of LGBTQ+ people and the concerns of, in particular, evangelical Christians. This struggle was captured by Anita Bryant's Save Our Children campaign that fought against then emerging nondiscrimination policies protecting "homosexuals." This campaign, while viewed as hateful by the left, was seen by Bryant as rooted in love. "I don't hate the homosexuals," Bryant (1977) claimed. "I love them enough to tell them the truth . . . that God hates sin but He loves the sinner and He will forgive any sin if the sinner repents of his sin . . . and not flaunt it or ask the law to condone it" To give in to the "agenda" of the radical militant homosexuals and their claims to legal rights would, by her estimation, "destroy the moral fiber of our families and our nation" (p. 104). Such rhetoric inflamed the debates, sedimenting, at least in the popular consciousness, a definition of religiousness that was (a) de facto politically conservative and (b) alongside abortion rights, animated by its anti-LGBTQ+ agenda. And there was a reverse impact on LGBTQ+ movements, including queer theory. As Melissa Sanchez (2019) aptly notes, "given that the rise of right-wing evangelicalism was coterminous with that of queer theory, it is unsurprising that the field [queer theory] tends to regard Christianity with suspicion, if not hostility" (pp. 8–9). The response by the sexually minoritized was understandable: a rearguard action that maintained its humanity and decoupled gay possibility, again at least publicly, from religion.

This came concurrently with a resurgence of a specific kind of masculine Christianity in the United States that, although it has a longer history than we're accounting for here, meant that a "resurgent militancy would become intertwined both with the sexual purity movement and with the assertion of complementarianism within evangelical circles" (du Mez, 2020, p. 172). This version of masculinity, which has seen its apotheosis in the full embrace of Donald Trump by evangelicals, was rooted in a ginned-up concern for "'soft males'" emerging from "'homosexual neurosis,'" due to both "addiction to pornography" and "the proliferation of androgynous gender roles" (p. 159). The answer was a muscular Jesus who could be used to assert that "most of life's obstacles could be overcome 'by exerting a little over ten pounds of pressure with a trigger finger'" (p. 217). We are, of necessity, telling a partial and streamlined story here. There are more detailed accounts that flesh out the production of American religious freedom through both conservative and progressive engagement in the public square (Curtis, 2016), just as there are gay and lesbian theological traditions that maintain space for, for instance, gender fluidity and sexual variety in religious spaces (Greenough, 2020), just as there are, as well, more thorough analyses of the racism inherent to American Evangelicalism historically (Butler, 2021). These tend to support our sense, however, that the general strand in engagement in public activism as in the last decades of social science was an antagonism between religion, read as conservative, and LGBTQ+ lives and theories.

The violence here is not limited to evangelicalism; certainly Catholicism, the tradition out of which Alison seeks to rework a new way forward for LGBTQ+ possibility with theology, has its own abhorrent history. We need only look to the die-ins at St. Patrick's in New York as a rebuttal to Cardinal O'Connor's public adoption of murderous tropes around HIV/AIDS in the 1980s to confirm this or, more contemporaneously, Martel's (2019) documentation of the operation and consequences of the "closet" in the Catholic Church. But the suggestion from Alison is that these responses are linked together by a misunderstanding of the structure and use of religious love as a violent act made manifest through a false God. His response, as we've noted, is to lower the temperature and to try to interrupt the cycle of abuse with an approach that can be understood, even if rejected by, religious conservatives while providing succor for both secular and religious progressives and sexual minorities.

On Liking

Liking, as we have come to conceptualize it, is intimately informed by Alison (2003) and his argument that "like" opens up in distinction from, for instance, love. Alison suggests that religious love is often wielded as a weapon that excludes the possibility of liking the other as other because it often "means something like: 'I feel that in obedience to God's love for sinners I must stop you being who you are'" (p. 107). We've written about this phenomenon as it gets applied in educational spaces—where it is quite common for teachers to suggest that they love their students—because much of the inevitable conclusion of teaching is that through schooling, students will be *made* to become different (Burke & Greteman, 2013). Our sense is that love, as engaged here, means very much a wedging of specific students into acceptable forms such that they might be produced as educated whereas liking means walking alongside students, accepting their curiosities, and failing to seek specific ends that existed prior to the meeting of the student. This, however, may be too clean a binary. Certainly not all educators, when they speak of their love for students, view them as sinners to be kept from the hands of an angry God, but there are good data that suggest that in the United States, with its uniquely religious teacher workforce (Hartwick, 2015b; White, 2009), a kind of love the sinners out of sin through punishment does, in fact, persist deeply and truly as a vein in the rock of American schooling (Hartwick, 2015a).

Hadley (2020) writes extensively about the kinds of struggles we attempt to work through here. In an account of three evangelical early-career teachers, the author-as-ethnographer documents the dilemmas that emerge for teachers who have been raised in religious discourses that demand a particular kind of love, especially from women. Hadley uses a Derridean frame rooted in hospitality, asking "how does one wholeheartedly welcome a guest or stranger . . . while remaining in power" (p. 40) to try to engage the difficulty for emerging teachers raised in certain kinds of evangelical (but not only evangelical) traditions when they encounter challenges to their faith in schools. Not surprisingly, much of the data emerge around issues of sexuality and gender identity. Noelle, one of the teachers, when thinking of a student, Hannah, who is in the midst of transitioning from female to male, speaks of her responsibility to the student and her faith in this way:

> Well, I'm responsible for making sure that my student feels loved
> and accepted. And I'm responsible to myself and my faith in God,
> and the fact that I believe that God created you in his image the way
> that you are and that's who you are supposed to be even if you might
> feel tensions to identify as somebody else. (p. 91)

Leaving aside very real concerns about notions of who gets to decide what a student is supposed to be, we can look at the difficulty and perhaps elegance of Noelle's solution when Hannah asks to be referred to with masculine pronouns. In answer, she says that, by way of support for the student, "it doesn't matter what you want to be called. You're still the same person no matter what your name is" (Hadley, 2020, p. 91). There's a way, if you squint at it, that the student could take this as a statement of support, and in fact, the student, who was very close with Noelle, did indeed take it that way. But the carefully crafted statement, for Noelle, maintains a kind of plausible deniability with reference to her faith and its belief in complementary and fixed gender roles to function as a teacher in the space. This isn't an apologia for Noelle's move, but it is meant to point to the use of love in educational spaces for religious ends while also holding out the notion that these are dilemmas that our teachers will face, indeed that their students will face as a result of their teachers' beliefs, with which we need to think in teacher education.

A second, more extreme example will help here. Mei Lin, another early-career evangelical teacher—who, it should be said, would see herself arising from different perhaps more Calvinist strands within the tradition than Noelle—speaks of times in her public school teaching when she fails to fully represent her faith. "I've gotten to the point where I don't even say, 'Sorry, God,' anymore" (Hadley, 2020, p. 109), her eyes filling with tears. "I'm panicked because I think I'm not saved" (p. 109). It's no surprise, then, that she rejects Noelle's "softer, less direct form of evangelism," noting,

> The way people have [evangelized] in the Bible has always been very explicit. . . . Every single time, like in every story, people are being very explicit with their words—almost rude—when they evangelize. And so I think if I'm basing [my sense of how to evangelize] on the model of how Jesus and his disciples did it, it would have to be with words. (p. 103)

There are easy ways to make a caricature out of Mei Lin, and so it's important to note that she does some extraordinary work for her students, including loaning $2,000 to one she notices is struggling to support his family with no expectation that he will pay her back. This puts her job on the line as it flouts district policy, but she sees it as a necessary support for a student in need and as a way to help him better engage in class so he won't have to work nights and can get some sleep. Certainly this is also driven by her faith as is, it's important to note, her very explicit antiracist pedagogy in the classroom.

Later, Mei Lin discusses her struggle to "support" LGBTQ+ students. She pays lip service to creating safe spaces for them but, in the end, knows that her faith means that if she doesn't bring them to Jesus, which would mean their acknowledging the sin of their identity and either becoming straight or pretending to, then she could go to hell and certainly her queer-identified students will. She, out of necessity for their shared salvation, must love them into something different. And, of course, this is violent, and of course, it's troubling,

but we do want to call to mind the deep belief for Mei Lin that eternal dam-
nation is *real* and that it will mean profound and endless suffering. And to be
absolutely clear—we don't endorse this position. We emerged from different
religious traditions that might be said to be a bit more humane, at least in the
last 70-odd years, regarding the afterlife. And we don't condone the need to
convert gay students in any way, but we bring forward Mei Lin to remind all
of us that teacher candidates (and eventual teachers) like her exist; they sit in
our courses; they pay lip service to our discussions of inclusion; they are a real
and not insignificant part of our public school–teaching cohort. So what ought
we do to work with them to both protect their future LGBTQ+ students and
help them think differently about what it means to teach amid the paradox of
pluralism (Paris, 2012)?

   We will not be able to offer an answer to what we ought to do that resolves
these issues once and for all. Rather, we hope to work through the needs teacher
educators have in responding to the range of issues that can arise when religious,
sexual, and gender identities meet in classrooms. Hadley's (2020) engagement
with evangelical teachers already illustrates that the issues are not the same but
refracted through a range of ideas and relations that fall under the banner of
evangelical Christianity. Her work illustrates, as well, the need to open up such
conversations and the challenges of doing so given the ways such issues raise
questions about one's conscience.

   For Alison (2003), "someone of unbound conscience can dare to get it
wrong, because they don't have to get it right" (p. 110). Yet, for many, if not
all of us, our consciences are bound in various ways—consciously or un-
consciously—due to our own conditions and contexts becoming subjects.
Additionally, within our current polarized environment, the consequences of
getting it wrong are serious, creating additional roadblocks to embarking on
conversations rooted in liking the other, conversations again not derived from
a need to change the other. This is not to argue that change is not possible but
to recognize that change cannot be the starting point directed from the outside. The teacher, for instance, cannot position themselves over-against their
students morally, even though this seems commonplace, whereby the teacher
is expected to "know" and be a moral exemplar. This "over-against" structures
the relation such that "it is the other who gets to stagger around the world as a
sinner, bearing the weight of 'my' morality" (p. 26). The violence that emerges

from this relation is rooted in distinctions between the pure and impure which are human creations and stories, not, in Alison's theological view, the divine. Talk of the divine and morality is complex in public education for many of the reasons we write of in this book. Yet in turning to such language—alongside other languages—is to tell different stories that are rooted in the diverse discourses and realities that undergird public education, the relations between students and teachers, and questions of citizenship.

We draw on Alison (2003) because he attempted, quite humbly, to begin to offer an alternative story to this form of relation that, in a sense, embraces shame. Shame becomes inhabitable by the other, by not desiring what is desired but allowing for other desires to challenge and create a different narrative. This, curiously, aligns with queer embraces of shame that similarly expose the ways normative logics fail at recognizing the plurality of human becoming. Alison's argument challenges dominant theological positions not by seeking entrance to that position but by showing that by inhabiting the position of shame one undoes the logic of goodness—a human logic, not a divine logic. If one's goodness is created by positioning the other as bad, one's goodness is exposed as, quite simply, a human invention informed by human desires and fears.

The ways in which LGBTQ+ individuals have been constructed by various religious discourses as sinful or in need of change explains, in part, we suspect why, according to the Pew Research Center, lesbian, gay and bisexual Americans were *less* likely than straight Americans to say churches protect and strengthen morality (Sandstrom & Schwadel, 2019). Relatedly, Pew Research also found that, while LGB Americans made up 5% of the respondents to their survey, they are "much less likely to say that scripture is the word of God" (38% of bisexuals, 33% of gays and lesbians, and 61% of straight Americans saying this; Schwadel & Sandstrom, 2019). Similarly, 34% of gays, lesbians, and bisexuals said religion is very important in their lives while more than half (54%) of straight Americans said religion is very important in their lives. These differences can illustrate a range of realities, and we think this range of realities deserves conversations that help unpack opportunities to relate differently to one another. Systems of goodness that prop up particular ideas of morality are never actually static, nor universal. Rather, morals are in flux as ideas and practices evolve and communities come into contact. For instance, over the past several decades, an overwhelming majority of U.S. adults have come to understand that they know someone who is gay, while most U.S. adults still do not know a transgender individual (Masci, 2016). Given this, Pew found that "nearly two-thirds of those who know a gay or lesbian person (64%) say homosexual behavior is either morally acceptable or not a moral issue, while about half (53%) of those who *don't* know a gay or lesbian person feel this way" (Masci, 2016, para. 7). And although we might peg these shifts precisely to the decline in religious membership in the United States alongside cultural and legislative wins for advocates of LGBTQ+ viability, we also still have significant gaps in belief that will inevitably play out in schools. Still, such changes in thinking are a reason why it is important to engage in conversations at these intersections within education where generations meet, come into presence, and engage in the work of learning.

A Case

Systems of goodness take on different flavors depending on how one's contexts and communities understand and view the world. Teachers and teacher educators have to navigate contexts and communities to make sense of such systems and enter into educational relations not only with students but other colleagues, parents, and community members as well. While Hadley's (2020) work touches on evangelical teachers, we end this chapter thinking about nominally secular teachers through an anecdote. This anecdote emerges from a conversation with an in-service teacher who asked for help navigating a situation that had emerged with a trans student. As teacher education scholars who explore realms of religion, gender, and sexuality, we often find ourselves fielding such questions and having conversations with not only our students but also other educators about, in this instance, gender identity. For those who position themselves as "theorists," in some way such moments can provoke mild annoyance as they request that theory leave its bracketed safety to encounter the particular. We have ourselves felt this mild annoyance. However, as we have continued our work and developed the arguments in this book, we have returned to such conversations, reseeing them for their potential, bringing abstract commitments into concrete practices. For each of us, such moments, on reflection, are exhilarating for the ways in which they recognize that we may, after all, have something to contribute to work "on the ground." Given the preceding conversation about the potential of liking the other, we turn to this particular conversation that we think offers a glimpse into a way one's teacher identity is always in process because of the students one teaches and the issues they bring to the classroom. This process is not easy but raises further questions and feelings, including questions about one's viability as a teacher and feelings of shame and annoyance.

There is, for us, little doubt that LGBTQ+ issues have gained an important foothold in education broadly speaking. Research on LGBTQ+ students, teachers, and curriculum has drastically expanded over the past several decades (Graves, 2015; Rodriguez et al., 2016; Rofes, 2005). For instance, laws mandating LGBTQ+ curricula have been expanding, as have various protections against discrimination and harassment (Biegel, 2010; Mayo, 2014). However, attention to LGBTQ+ issues within teacher education remains complicated as such attention is more dependent on the context of the teacher education program that creates challenges for in-service teachers who can enter classrooms without any preparation about how to navigate a range of issues related to gender and sexuality.

In LGBTQ+ conversations in education, there has been an evolution around the work of the "ally." Within the history of the ever-expanding acronym, and its contestations, the "A" once stood for "ally" recognizing those heterosexuals who fought/struggled/joined alongside LGBTQ+ people. The "A" has evolved in the 21st century to shed its "ally" meaning and now more consistently refers to "Asexual." This comes alongside the ways in which the concept of the ally has been challenged in recent years to do more than merely "ally" but, instead, become an "accomplice" or "co-conspirator." Each of these alternatives articulates a demand that one must do more than be an "ally" linked to an assumption that there is a certain incompleteness to the commitments required of allyship. This shift, seen in broader social justice discourses, comes with the recognition, for instance, that action is required, indeed that one must put oneself at risk in ways that perhaps were not demanded in the past. How such discourses play out on the ground, we suspect, is far more complicated around how risk is encountered and experienced since how one identifies may not be as visible as how one performs and is identified by others who may have ill will.

Curiously, this evolution implicates the realities of change and how such change bears out across generations. We cannot claim by any means that schools are a safe place for LGBTQ+ students (Meyer, 2009; Sadowski, 2016). Research continues to document the harassment, bullying, and violence that LGBTQ+ students face in disproportionate numbers, including at the hands of teachers (Kosciw et al., 2018). Yet we do know that more and more teachers—still a minority most likely—are taking up the work of anti-homophobia not only through everyday actions, for sure, but also through advising Gay-Straight Alliances and seeking out ways to provide other, more substantial modes of support. Such supports are, unfortunately, often rooted in particular understandings of LGBTQ+ lives. In a conversation with an in-service teacher, this complexity manifested itself. She, a cisgender female high school teacher, raised questions about how to support trans and nonbinary students. Attentive to their needs around both privacy and recognition, along with the legal landscapes that remain unsettled and contingent based on state and district policy, she expressed a feeling of being caught in an impossible place.

Her trans and nonbinary students had access to political discourses as they emerged and evolved most notably on various social media platforms. They were, in many ways, trying on such ideas to help make sense of their own emerging identities that were becoming in relationship to others in ways social media allows. Unlike trans and nonbinary youth a few years ago, she noted, youth were bringing in critical terms to assert their selves; this a good thing. This, also, an important part of high school itself, has made it more complicated and dangerous for trans and nonbinary students given the backlash against trans rights and the contested realities that trans and nonbinary students face as they navigate what should otherwise be the quotidian: bathrooms, pronouns, clothing (Coupet & Marrus, 2015). And she was, in working with the students, put in a challenging position of both supporting them but pushing them to recognize the complications in play. For instance, a trans student accused her of being transphobic for asking the student how they would like her to refer to them when talking with their parents. Unsure if or how the student was out to parents, she wanted to be sure to protect their privacy while also being mindful of their relationship with family. The student, however, felt that these were settled issues and being asked at all was inconsiderate, at best, and transphobic, at worse.

What this case illustrates—in condensed form—is not the need to decide what is and is not transphobia, although that is a needed, important, and always contingent project as dynamics change. Rather, what it reveals for us are the challenges of meeting in schools where these discourses are not abstract but concretely present and constantly evolving. Adam's response to the teacher was, in part, to think through with her what it might mean to like that student, to accompany them through those discourses and what they mean in everyday educational relations. How do students coming into themselves understand concepts like transphobia such that engaging in such conversations can assist in fleshing out that concept for students in relation to teachers? It was clear that the accusation of transphobia hit the teacher personally. She wanted to work through if or how her actions indeed were transphobic. But she also had to think through how to relate to the student moving forward, remembering as well that the student is themself on the rocky road of becoming. The student may have, at least momentarily, hated their teacher. And that teacher may have, as well, hated the student not for their transness but for their adolescence. We return to notions of hate in Chapter 5 but, for now, want to sit with its affective possibility and pain. The affective realities of classrooms are charged after all, made challenging, we suggest, when we err toward love and hate as extreme feelings. A point here is the need to have conversations through these terrains that are simultaneously abstract and concrete.

Conclusion

Liking the other, we hope, offers us a framework to think through the challenges that arise when people meet both in teacher education classrooms and preK–12 classrooms given the ways they are intimately implicated in one another. As we address in later chapters, liking the other creates a way to both explore our own conscience and engage the consciences of others who are similarly amid their own becoming. In liking the other, however, we do not offer a prescription for relations but a different story for how we might relate to ourselves and others. The burden of liking may fall at first on teachers who establish the relational mood in classrooms. However, the self is never independent of the other; rather, the other is vitally important to our abilities to become a self. So liking quickly becomes multidirectional in recognizing the relations in play. Liking, we propose, provides an alternative, arguably simpler, perhaps more mundane, way of conceiving our relations. Such relations, however, are never simple. In public education, they are, as well, wrapped up within legal discourses that form and reform the rights students and teachers have (and don't have) as they pass through the schoolhouse doors. The remainder of the book is a rumination on concepts through which we might think engagement across religious, sexuality, and gender discourses in education. We turn first to prophetic indictment to understand barriers to the work and then move to legal histories as a way to establish both context and an argument, later, that lead us away from accommodation and the juridical. Along the way, we consider twinned notions of forgiveness and reconciliation as a way to build toward accompaniment as a culmination of liking across these various conceptual arguments.

References

Alison, J. (2003). *On being liked*. Herder & Herder.

Biegel, S. (2010). *The right to be out: Sexual orientation and gender identity in America's public schools*. University of Minnesota Press.

Blumberg, A. (2017, April 6). New analysis finds Clinton, not Trump narrowly won the Catholic vote in 2016. *Huffington Post*. https://www.huffpost.com/entry/new-analysis-finds-clinton-not-trump-narrowly-won-the-catholic-vote-in-2016_n_58e574bce4b06a4cb30f0aaf

Bryant, A. (1977). *When the homosexuals burn the Holy Bible in public ... How can I stand by silently*. Anita Bryant Ministries.

Burke, K. J., & Greteman, A. J. (2013). Toward a theory of liking. *Educational Theory*, 63(2), 151–170.

Burke, K. J., & Greteman, A. J. (2020). Educating tensions between religious and sexuality discourses: On resentment and hospitality. *Review of Education, Pedagogy, and Cultural Studies*, 43(1), 49–68.

Butler, A. (2021). *White evangelical racism: The politics of morality in America*. Ferris and Ferris.

Coupet, S., & Marrus, E. (Eds.). (2015). *Children, sexuality, and the law*. NYU Press.

Curtis, F. (2016). *The production of American religious freedom*. NYU Press.

Du Mez, K. K. (2020). *Jesus and John Wayne: How White evangelicals corrupted a faith and fractured a nation*. Liveright Publishing Corporation.

Graves, K. (2015). LGBTQ education research in historical context. In G. Wimberly (Ed.), *LGBTQ issues in education: Advancing a research agenda* (pp. 23–42). AERA.

Greenough, C. (2020). *Queer theologies*. Routledge.

Greteman, A. J., & Burke, K. J. (2017). *The pedagogies and politics of liking*. Routledge.

Hadley, H. L. (2020). *Navigating moments of hesitation: Portraits of evangelical English language arts teachers*. Myers Education Press.

Haraway, D. (2016). *Staying with the trouble: Making kin in the Chthulucene.* Duke University Press.

Harris, S. (2005). *The end of faith: Religion, terror and the future of reason.* W. W. Norton & Company.

Hartwick, J. (2015a). Public school teachers' beliefs in and conceptions of God: What teachers believe, and why it matters. *Religion & Education, 42*(2), 1–25.

Hartwick, J. (2015b). Teacher prayerfulness: Identifying public school teachers who connect their spiritual and religious lives with their professional lives. *Religion & Education, 42*(1), 54–80.

Heyes, J. M. (In press). *Sexuality education as political theology: Pathways to nonviolence.* Sex Education.

Hitchens, C. (2007). *God is not great: How religion poisons everything.* Hachette.

Jakobsen, J. R., & Pellegrini, A. (Eds.). (2008). *Secularisms.* Duke University Press.

Kosciw, J. G., Greytak, E. A., Zongrone, A. D., Clark, C. M., & Truong, N. L. (2018). *The 2017 National School Climate Survey: The experiences of lesbian, gay, bisexual, transgender, and queer youth in our nation's schools.* GLSEN.

Martel, F. (2019). *In the closet of the Vatican: Power, homosexuality, hypocrisy.* Bloomsbury/Continuum.

Masci, D. (2016, September 28). *Key findings about Americans' views on religious liberty and nondiscrimination.* Pew Research Center. https://www.pewresearch.org/fact-tank/2016/09/28/key-findings-about-americans-views-on-religious-liberty-and-nondiscrimination/

Mayo, C. (2014). *LGBTQ youth and education: Policies and practices.* Teachers College Press.

Meyer, E. (2009). *Gender, bullying, and harassment: Strategies to end sexism and homophobia in schools.* Teachers College Press.

Paris, D. (2012). Culturally sustaining pedagogy: A needed change in stance, terminology, and practice. *Educational Researcher, 41*(3), 93–97.

Pulliam, S., & Olsen, T. (2008, January 23). Q&A: Barack Obama. *Christianity Today.* https://www.christianitytoday.com/ct/2008/januaryweb-only/104-32.0.html

Putnam, R. D., & Campbell, D. E. (2010). *American grace: How religion divides and unites us.* Simon & Schuster.

Rasmussen, M. L. (2016). *Progressive sexuality education: The conceits of secularism.* Routledge.

Rodriguez, N. M., Martino, W. J., Ingrey, J. C., & Brockenbrough, E. (Eds.). (2016). *Critical concepts in queer studies and education.* Palgrave Macmillan.

Rofes, E. (2005). *A radical rethinking of sexuality and schooling: Status quo or status queer?* Rowman & Littlefield.

Sadowski, M. (2016). *Safe is not enough: Better schools for LGBTQ students.* Harvard Education Press.

Sanchez, M. (2019). *Queer faith: Reading promiscuity and race in the secular love tradi-tion*. NYU Press.

Sandstrom, A., & Schwadel, P. (2019, June 12). *Lesbian, gay, and bisexual Americans are more critical of churches than straight adults are*. Pew Research Center. https://www.pewresearch.org/fact-tank/2019/06/13/lesbian-gay-and-bisexual-amer-icans-are-more-critical-of-churches-than-straight-adults-are/

Schwadel, P., & Sandstrom, A. (2019, May 24). *Lesbian, gay, and bisexual Americans are less religious than straight adults by traditional measures*. Pew Research Center. https://www.pewresearch.org/fact-tank/2019/05/24/lesbian-gay-and-bisexu-al-americans-are-less-religious-than-straight-adults-by-traditional-measures/

Taylor, C. (2011). Why we need a radical redefinition of secularism. In E. Mendieta & J. Vanantwerpen (Eds.), *The power of religion in the public sphere* (pp. 34–59). Columbia University Press.

White, K. R. (2009). Connecting and teacher identity: The unexplored relationship between teachers and in public schools. *Teaching and Teacher Education, 25*(7), 857–866.

CHAPTER 3

Prophetic Indictment And The Limits of Discourse And Community Understanding

A Preliminary Conversation

Kevin: I remember very few homilies from growing up. This isn't all that surprising given the peripatetic attention span of a kid forced to go to Mass every Sunday (as well as on Catholic Holy Days of Obligation, which are like boredom wild cards in the deck of any given calendar year; hey . . . more time in the pew!) until he left for college. Some of that, probably, has to do with the way in which preaching isn't necessarily stressed in the training of Catholic priests (Dominicans aside), at least as far as I can tell, in comparison to some of the more flamboyant or doctrinaire Protestant denominations. Certainly we never got anything quite so interesting nor fiery as that which emerges from the prophetic tradition in certain strands of Black churches. The one sermon—a word we never used for whatever reason—I do remember came later in my high school years. By that point, my mom's parish had been led by the same pastor for more than a decade. This was relatively rare in dioceses at the time as priests were supposed to be rotated throughout the city every seven years, the idea being to offer different contexts in which a person might serve, I suppose. One could, however, apply for extensions, and Fr. Tilrock had made St. Barnabas his home and had no intention of leaving prior to retirement. He had been, at the start of his term, overly shy. This caused trouble as his predecessor had been much loved, in large part, because he was gregarious in the kind of hail-fellow-well-met way that made parish politics navigable for a certain kind of post-ethnic White population in the 1990s. All fundraising and ladies' club meetings and avoiding connecting the dots too explicitly on condemnations of racism that might emerge from Gospel readings. Tilrock, however, . . . he was perhaps more committed to the faith in an institutional sense than he was to being the sort of

ward politician that a priest might need to be on the White South Side of Chicago
to win over hearts and wallets. Then, suddenly, he got a dog—for whom he bought
boots ("Boots!" laughed my costive mother) to spare the mutt from the salt and
snow of winters—and, through his frequent neighborhood walks, over the years
started to build a rapport and political clout among the faithful.

He was uncontroversial, however, that was certainly his brand. He was bland
and gentle and kind. He came to graduation parties and left early; he brought
Communion to the homebound; he walked his dog down to parish soccer games
and then holed up in the rectory on the hill to drink tea and read, I imagine.
When he spoke at Mass, he reflected on the scriptural readings of a given day, as
all priests are supposed to do, and stayed, almost ostentatiously in his avoidance,
away from social issues.

The homily I remember, however, was emotional. It seems his brother had
recently died. And his brother was gay and openly so, which back then was perhaps less common or at least certainly less spoken about in the circles in which
I'd been raised. The homily was about the quotidian life his brother had lived,
special mostly to his family, and the harrowing saga they went through trying
to bury him in a Catholic cemetery. This from a pastor who couldn't find a plot
in supposedly sacred ground in Indiana to lay his beloved brother to rest. The
anger and anguish of the man on the altar were riveting, although his delivery
was plaintive. How, he asked, can we treat each other like this? How can the
church treat its gay children this way? It can't if it is to continue.

That was the first, and only, time that I'd encountered a homily that thought
in complex ways about sexuality and its attendant humanity before. Certainly
there were apologias for the wonders of marriage and the "fruits" of those marriages, but there wasn't much of anything about the particular complications of,
say, the families we sat near with their 10 children, everyone threadbare in one
way or another. The closest I'd ever gotten in my formal Catholic schooling was
in Confraternity of Christian Doctrine when Sr. Suzanne, older, matronly, told
us precocious fourth graders that the phrase "make love" was inaccurate because
only God could make love. That one stuck for some reason in ways that still
disturb me. Otherwise, we got reflections on Mary's virginity which, while send-
ing powerful messages about female sexuality, certainly, never really landed as
discussions of *human* possibility. She was mythical in ways Fr. Tilrock's brother
never could be. Here was a man mourning loss in his life as well as the pain and

anger of realizing the ways in which the church he seemed to love had hated his brother, indeed hated him even after death.

Adam: Stories like you just shared break my heart as they illustrate the human suffering that happens when sexuality and religion—Catholic here—meet at the level of "persons." Priests, particularly parish priests, work intimately at the level of persons with less time to engage in the work of doctrine. Or, put differently, priests see the work of doctrine, good and bad, as it is borne out on parishioners and broader publics. I suppose there is a parallel between parish priests and teachers in that both are tasked with "caring"—priests care for the flock, pastoring to the people while teachers care for students, teaching future generations. Both parties are usually so invested in building relations and working with others whom they have less time to invest in other work or forms of relations. This, for me, is important as it recognizes the limits of time in practice and the challenges it takes for anyone, foreshadowing an issue in an upcoming chapter, to "consider everything." This is particularly true given that things seem to change "on the ground" much faster than they do "in the clouds"—to create a problematic binary. I cannot help but imagine the struggle for a parish priest as he's faced with, what I will think of as, the violence of Catholic doctrine amid his own personal grief. When we meet such violence face-to-face, I suspect we might respond in various ways from considering things anew, doubling down on the doctrine, or suffering in silence. There seems, from your retelling, a certain grace in his response that remained while he shared that very real challenge with his parishioners. I think it is a moment of pastoring to, caring for one's flock in a way that implicates the self and makes the self vulnerable to others. I would be curious if you remember this sermon, in part, because it was a rare moment in which a parish priest made himself vulnerable or if it was more for the ways gayness emerged for parishioners?

I cannot recall a similar compelling moment with a sermon, probably because I tried to get out of going to church throughout my upbringing—and, strangely, had a devout grandmother who supported my resistance, perhaps because it allowed me to spend time with her. Rather, your story returned me to a similar scene steeped in disappointment, but a scene that also informs this book. It was a lecture given at Creighton University by Catholic theologian and priest James Alison, with whom we engage throughout this book. The lecture titled "Collapsing the Closet in the House of God" caused quite a stir in the mid-2000s, pitting a rather conservative archdiocese against a mildly progressive Jesuit university over a lecture on "homosexuality." Despite the controversy and protestations prior to the event, the lecture went on as scheduled. Alison (2005) notes at the outset of his talk what were most likely the competing interested parties in play, stating:

> There may be some here for whom a talk with a title like the one I have been invited to speak to sounds a bit like an invitation to a Big Bad Wolf to huff and puff and blow a house down. Some of you may be hoping that the closet in the House of God has been built by the wisest and holiest of pigs so as to resist such lupine breath as mine. While others think it quite time that the little pigs in question were either taken to market, or swept along in a Gadarene rush down some escarpment into some suitably accommodating sea. These others are hoping for ringside seats at the collapse. (para. 2)

Yet, all these parties would, in his estimation, be disappointed for he was out of breath. His work would not do what others imagined or fantasized; it might do for better or for worse. Rather, Alison breaths a different approach to life, "the breath of the lamb. The lamb standing as one slaughtered, whose breath is commonly known as the Holy Spirit. That, I suspect, is the only breath powerful enough for the work at hand" (2005, para. 3). That work was, in very related ways to our work, to tell a different story about the relationship between "religion" and "sexuality." And there in a lecture hall, I remember being transfixed by what I think of as a rather queer move—of moving to the side of binary oppositions—to do something else, to breathe life into a stale argument. There was for me, in Alison's lecture, which I return to often, a need to reread the word and therefore the world that such a reading did not merely swap places (e.g., the oppressed becomes the oppressor) but the power of voluntarily taking the place of the curse. I suspect we might need to unpack that further in concrete terms, but I think the idea opens up ways to think differently about the work of understanding others when "shared" understandings seem impossible. For our purposes then, I am curious how we name the ways our current moment— polarized as it is—makes it difficult to hear the other, which, in turn, makes it easier to "indict" the other on our own terms. In naming this, I wonder how we move to the side of such practices within education, drawing on Arendt, to both usher students into the world while not foreclosing their potential in transforming it.

Kevin: We have, for some time now in our collaborations, been writing of our desire to argue to the side of controversies. This started in our work on liking vis-à-vis loving in education and was rooted in a few of Alison's books. He's been a truly generative fellow traveler in this; still, I don't know that we've gotten much traction for our sense that choosing a side to reinforce when at loggerheads just means more concussive trauma for those involved. Of course, that oversimplifies things and flattens the way in which material realities are implicated by the struggles for life, recognition, and often even intelligibility differently affect certain individuals and their bodies. But what we've been trying to figure out most is how—embedded as we have been in a religious tradition that speaks often of being "prophets of a future not our own"—to help our respective fields, most especially teacher education, understand just how much of that religious rhetoric has become interlaced in its theories of how education might well "save" the world. This even as teacher educators constantly warn of the dangers of saviorism. What we wonder about, I think, is the sense that a prophetic tradition continues in education in ways underappreciated, and just how that then requires certain kinds of condemnation until we start to run out of steam, as Latour (2004) has written, or out of breath, as Alison (2005) noted. Perhaps we can find other sources of oxygen, then.

A Beginning

We begin with hatred. This is, in some ways, both too obvious and too opaque. It is easy to argue that much of the rift that has been produced by Christian religious discourse, and Christianity broadly conceived, has been rooted in a hatred generally of sin, such as it is, and particularly of sexual sin. It's easy enough, here, to stop pretending that such sin isn't attached to human bodies; this is about hatred of certain kinds of people. That is to say, religion has orchestrated a context in which hate produces its object: the specter of the gay and more recently the trans individual. This is well-tread ground (e.g., Pascoe, 2007) in the social sciences and LGBTQ+ studies and rightly so. In taking the discussion up, however, we think it first vital to assert the ways in which we ought to consider hatred not as the opposite of love but as its simulacrum (Yanay, 2013, p. 90). This can be surfaced in the kind of tossed-off rhetoric that exists in certain circles about hating the sin and not the sinner. Of course, when we accept the sin as ingrained in the very being of the sinner, the distinction clearly lacks a difference. And besides, as Alison (2001, 2003) readily reminds us, much of the modernist construction of religious love lies in the production of a subject primarily forgiven, which is to say mired in sin and requiring a benevolent confessor who, in turn, relies on that very sin for its own subsistence.

Love, as the forgiveness of sin in Christian rhetoric, then, requires hatred of the individual inasmuch as it remains rooted in a "love full of hatred" (Yanay, 2013, p. 13) and its counterpart a "hatred full of love." Just as the confessor requires confession to validate his own righteousness, so, too, does the love called on to grant such forgiveness require not only the pageantry of the process (Foucault, 2014) but also the hatred of the other (as manifesting sinfulness) for its fulfillment. This is about the production of obedience, yes (Foucault, 2008, p. 320), but also the very "system of juridical order" (Foucault, 2014, p. 180) that required the avowal of the truth of the self as fallen in order to maintain its power, through confession. This very avowal, both a sacramental and a sovereign rite, conditions the "guilty party" to provide "a foundation for his judges to condemn him" while he "recognizes his own will in the decision of the judges" (p. 207). Hate the sinner, hate the sin; get the sinner to hate themselves. And this hatred sits at the boundary of the breakdown between the self and other necessitating the construction of the abject, lest that boundary be revealed as permeable as it really is (Kristeva, 1982). The question then becomes, for Yanay (2013), and for us here, "what does hatred want" (p. 6) not only of the abject but as broadly conceived as well? In one sense, as we're thinking about it, hatred wants an other, close enough to love-and-hate. This chapter first examines the codependence of these loves full of hatred as made manifest through the supposed rift—reconceived, across the hyphens, as a bridge—and not only thinks about the discourses that produce such twinned maintenance of separation as connection but also offers, perhaps, a different and, we think, more interesting way forward.

One of the barriers to this work, particularly in the United States, comes from a long historico-rhetorical history rooted in prophetic indictment and its attendant expression, the Jeremiad. Kaveny (2016) argues that political impasses as they exist currently, especially ones that remain rutted—as with the logger-heads that often exist in schools over religion and queer existence—come about because of a discursive frame that encases American approaches to civil and social problems. That frame, linked to juridical Puritan traditions of prophetic indictment, carries forth in arguments about and around "controversial" topics; the assumption, first, is that a speaker (or writer or teacher educator or student teacher, for instance) has the ultimately divine thrust of communal moral agreement from which to call those in disagreement to repent and return to the fold. Kaveny (2016) writes that "those deploying the rhetoric of prophetic indictment tend to see their opponents as threatening the basic foundations of the social order which also serve as the foundations for calm and reasoned moral discourse" (p. 120). At its most basic level, the "jeremiad is centrally designed to lodge an indictment" which, it's important to note, is a juridical stance assuming that there is "no need to argue that the class of behavior it is condemning is objectionable" (p. 172). This presumption of shared values extends to the jeremiad which "presupposes general agreement on the requirements of the covenant" (p. 229) that binds a community. This was a primary mode by which Puritan sermonizing was conducted; Kaveny chronicles its bleed into supposedly secular political realms through the Civil War and beyond. The point is that one of the reasons that religious and queer discourses remain in opposition is largely because a call for detente misses the prophetic positioning out of which each community argues its points. Given that a shared moral universe, in the way that the Puritanical construction requires, with a looming, vengeful God on whose account a single speaker can chastise a united community, no longer exists (if it ever did), the jeremiad to return to godly ways or to abandon them fails to persuade. We're all prophets raging at the rising tide, in essence, and no one has developed ears to listen as everyone else has turned to salt.

The reader will recognize the implications such an analysis has for controversial political topics, most especially as this sort of thing plays out amid concerns around cancel culture and attacks on the supposed excesses of liberal, mostly affluent, college campuses. That there exists no shared moral or ethical understanding around the acceptability of actions that might be, for instance, considered cultural appropriation in some circles, ensures that when controversies occur around inappropriate Halloween costumes or changing expectations around language choices, no satisfactory conclusion can be reached. It's not that condemnation of violent acts is wrong; certainly this isn't the case. It's that such condemnation, even when appropriate, is (a) not understood as emerging from good-faith applications of moral principles and (b) most often seeks to condemn without the possibility for reconciliation. Given that we must reconcile ourselves to the students who enter our teacher education classrooms, condemnation often is both necessary and most often insufficient when encountering religious intolerance of LGBTQ+ identities, individuals, and traditions. Theological engagement through queer lenses, however, allows for a different approach.

What We Are Doing/What We Are Not Doing

An anecdote might be helpful in setting the terms of the foregoing discussion. Kevin edited a book series on Catholic education that sought to spur a movement toward critical, postmodern, and, indeed, queer work in the field. He recently had a conversation with a diocesan theologian[1] who has written a pedagogical text for teachers in Catholic schools. The theologian couldn't find an outlet for his work for lack of understanding from various publishers of pedagogical texts that an audience, and thus a market, exists for such a book. Most educational trade publishers fail to see Catholic schools as a viable market for texts; most Catholic publishers fail to publish pedagogical texts as they are much more focused on theological and pastoral questions; that education is considered outside these realms is a discussion for another time. The series seemed a likely home because of this particular donut hole in the publishing world. In the course of discussions about the text, however, the stuck point for the theologian was the series' affiliation with queer theory, which he'd not much read and feared might only position itself at the negative pole of his work. The portion of the description of the series that's germane to our concerns read: "Titles will approach the problem of a nuanced Catholic educational project drawing upon cultural studies, critical theories, feminist, queer, post-structural, new materialist, post humanist and/or curriculum studies lenses." This will, for many readers here, seem like a pretty standard list of potential stances by which one might conduct research in the social sciences and particularly in education. What's striking, of course, is that out of that list, the theologian found the word *queer*, and it affected him.

Much of what we're trying to do with this book is think about the fear that was present in this individual's voice, in considering the kind of repercussions that might come from, presumably, conservative critics who found he'd published a book in a series that mentioned queer research approaches though his pedagogical text drew on very different research traditions to do its work. But we also want to think about what's lost in other spaces where work engaging religion, even if queerly, can be dismissed out of hand, too. Ugena Whitlock (2006) plumbs these depths in her work, trying to make sense of the tensions that emerge as a lesbian woman raised fundamentalist Christian in the southern United States who maintains an interest in, and is drawn to, faith by her commitment to spiritual, if perhaps also religious work. She begins with an anecdote:

> "You can't be queer and a fundamentalist." That was what seemed to me a dismissive rejection of my submission by the editor of a prominent curriculum journal. The editor seemed to object to my reluctance to scathingly and utterly renounce the ideals and practices of fundamentalist Protestantism, the first and only Christian faith I have ever known. I suspect the editor's concern was compounded by my writing as a 'queer theorist' focused a bit too fondly on "Old Time Religion." (Whitlock, 2006, p. 65)

Not to belabor the point, but, of course, one can be queer and a fundamentalist, just as one can be a queer theorist and find ways to reconcile, as we argue later, queer theory with a fondness for, while maintaining a critical stance in relation to, religion. Still, the incommensurability of these two assumptions, of the theologian and the journal editor, mark the boundaries of our concerns here, and they remain rooted in a jeremiadic understanding of how the world, and its work, functions which we wish to trouble.

One concern with the work in this book might be that we are attempting to flatten power relations in such a way as to suggest that calls for a kind of reconciliation will require equal flesh on the scale from religious and queer discourses or, more likely, religious and queer persons. Call it an all-lives-matter kind of move: Everyone needs to find common ground, give up some on their rigidly held ideals, and all will be well because there's clearly equal blame all around. This is both patently untrue and uniquely unhelpful for our thinking.

What we do want to suggest, however, is that there are approaches to religion and theology—traditions and writings that emerge from both spaces—that might be both helpful to queer thinking and theorizing along with making queer lives differently possible most especially in schools. We won't, either, claim any manner of panacea here. One pitfall to this kind of work lies in falling into a practice of proof-texting that would suggest, as did Steven Paulikas (2017) that "only good theology can debunk bad theology" (para. 10). It's easy enough to see the problems with such a statement as it relies on inherently subjective definitions, malleable ones, of what is good and bad, but more important, it suggests that there is some secret key that we might somehow find that will open the door to the good just as it bars the way, once we're through, to the bad.

With Alison (2003), we're patently uninterested in the construction of good and bad in this case and choose rather, as we have in other spaces, to argue to the side, taking the narrow gate, in the direction of something different. And so while it's in some ways tempting to pull from documents like Frédéric Martel's (2019) book on homosexuality in the Vatican by citing, for instance, a rereading of Aquinas in which "homosexuality," rather than being intrinsically disordered as is "official" doctrinal Catholic teaching, actually "does not bear within it illicitness, and as to its origin, natural to the individual and rooted in what animates him as a human being, and as to its aim, loving another person, which is a good aim" (p. 105). We might, similarly, draw on Salzman and Lawler's (2008) work and suggest a newly considered Catholic anthropology of sexuality that demands no condemnation of queer sexual sin as inherent to religious faith, instead turning to "virtue ethics" that "does not focus primarily on actions" but "asks another set of questions: who are we? Who are we striving to become? How do we get there?" (p. 118). But these critiques, useful though they may be, are vulnerable to opposing hermeneutic responses from more conservative realms. Still, we think this focus on becoming and the how of our getting there is worth holding up as a way forward: Where might we go, thinking across religious and queer discourses, absent our proclivity for the easy indictment of the jeremiad?

Rather, where we want to go lies in the sense of split camps, failing to argue in common terms and thus missing the opportunities for different thinking within their own conversations. We're intrigued by the possibilities inherent in dialogue, in conversation. Peace (2001), in a chapter on the ongoing sociocultural project of the production of lesbian identities, suggests that "a dialogic space of encounter is engendered when emancipatory claims contest policy" (p. 37). We're not particularly sanguine about the project of emancipatory practices in work that's rooted in queer theory, but we do think there are new forms of encounter possible in the emergence of and through dialogue. This kind of dialogic ethos for Kinloch and San Pedro (2014) is imagined as a spiral of call-and-response characterized most fruitfully through "openly listen[ing] to what is said and not said" (p. 28), "allowing room for conflict, complications, silences, and pauses to exist" (p. 29). Opening space for dialogue, both in the structure of this book and in the junction point between queer and religious discourses, might mean both new possibilities and new practices. This is to say that because of how prophetic indictment functions, queer theorists fail to engage fruitfully with theological texts and miss, then, a richness of theory that might inform robust thinking going forward, not to engage, necessarily, with religious readers nor to change their minds—although that's perhaps possible when we, suddenly, experience a shift in the sacred—but in order to enliven, to enrich their own thinking.

The Wrath of History

Turning backward to a moment where religion and queer lives were, in a sense, at a pinnacle of animosity and antagonism, namely, the AIDS pandemic, we might find an opening. This opening is generative on a number of fronts. First, as Sarah Schulman (2012) articulates, there has been a certain gentrification of the mind around HIV/AIDS, which has contributed to a loss of collective memory. This is inherently an educational issue that asks, as Schulman did, "Do they know their own history? Do they wonder why there are so few sixty-year-old versions of themselves passing by on the sidewalk?" (p. 63). Such an educational question is not, however, purely about the past but about how the past bleeds into the present reminding us, as artist and AIDS activist Gregg Bordowitz proclaimed, "The AIDS crisis is still beginning" (Truett, 2019). Second, there has been a return to the HIV/AIDS pandemic's past—in what Avram Finkelstein (2018) calls AIDS 2.0—that is, retelling the complicated stories of that history in our present. It is within this context of AIDS 2.0 that thinking anew about the complex relationship between queers and religions might make palpable the need for such work and its unfinished realities.

Jonathan Silin (1995) argues that the age of AIDS brought forward "our passion for ignorance" in education (p. 3). Amid a global health pandemic, HIV/AIDS illustrated not only the limits of knowledge but also the need to understand "how we agree *not* to know" (p. 9). This willed not-knowing refused to engage what we did know, primarily through the tireless work of AIDS activists who challenged the scientific and medical establishment's neglect and slowness in responding to the initial crisis. This work highlighted, as Silin notes, that "medical knowledge is not discovered but constructed, not objectively out there, a reflection of physical reality, but socially negotiated to enhance an arbitrary set of economic arrangements and distribution of power" (p. 19). Instead, throughout the first decades of the pandemic, blame and embarrassment were the preferred responses to, in particular, supposed "guilty parties" (e.g., gay men, IV drug users, and sex workers). This turn to blame and embarrassment—with lethal consequences—was, in part, rooted in moralistic jingoism that sought to protect the "family" and "national body." This was made visible as AIDS activists pushed against particular institutions—scientific and medical for sure as seen in protests against the National Institutes of Health and pharmaceutical companies—but also notably the Catholic Church.

The Catholic Church was by no means the only religious institution or faith tradition at odds with AIDS activism. These histories at the collision point between AIDS activists and religious organizations are more complicated. However, to complicate such stories is not to ignore a key reality that involved the work of prophetic indictment by religious leaders. As Petro (2015) illustrates, HIV/AIDS was constructed less as a public health pandemic than as a moral one. Religious leaders of the 1980s and 1990s helped draw the lines— battle lines by and large—between sex and religion that continue to shape the pandemic. The high-profile stories that emerged during the 1980s framed a set of issues that continue to haunt the histories of AIDS and the work of accountability on behalf of those lost. This includes, for instance, Jerry Falwell's notorious pronouncement that "AIDS was God's punishment for homosexuals" (see Kohler, 2020). And this wrath was directed at not only homosexuals but also societies that tolerated homosexuality. Of course, such wrath was not entirely new but, rather, called on longer histories of religious perceptions of sexuality, such as sodomy, which itself has been complicated by theological exploration (Jordan, 1998).

The prophetic indictment from religious leaders contributed to, in large part, the hardening of battle lines and the perception that religion was only ever at odds with certain forms of sexuality. Yet, as Petro (2015) documented, "this perception has fueled narratives of gay and lesbian history that overlook the long record of religious entanglement with homosexuality, including at times support for gay and lesbian rights" (p. 14). Put differently, there is a need to reexamine these perceptions in order to think both historically about the complicated stories of HIV/AIDS and to move forward with a different set of perceptions. Petro's work itself contributes to this project, particularly as he illustrated that "as a theological crisis, AIDS forced religious individuals to confront their stances on issues such as homosexuality, leading some to revise theologies that considered it sinful" (p. 35). Such work, we believe, is easier said than done as it requires that we wrestle with the traumatic impact such perceptions have had on queers of various generations, provide opportunities to learn a history still largely absent from U.S. education, and teach such history and its contemporary import in complicated ways. Our work in this book is but an initial attempt to think through such potential by addressing some of the layers of issues in play, from legal landscapes to the work of identity and paradoxes of forgiveness and hospitality—all of this, again, within teacher education where future teachers encounter the work of learning and unlearning the pedagogical and curricular needs of future students. Pandemics—here HIV/AIDS, as well as COVID-19—raise serious questions about education, its limits, and more for all involved.

The perception that religion and LGBTQ+ people are at odds, a perception solidified during the first decade and a half of the AIDS pandemic, cannot be the only perception. The intense divide between LGBTQ+ discourses and religious discourses remains quite fraught. Demographics and surveys illustrate a shifting ground, proclamations by Pope Francis have provided glimpses of hope to lesbian and gay Catholics while scapegoating trans Catholics, and various faith traditions have expanded possibilities for LGBTQ+ individuals. This shifting ground, of course, remains active with the *responsum* by the Congregation for the Doctrine of the Faith (CDF) on denying Catholic priests' ability to bless same-sex unions in the spring of 2021. Here, we see, Catholics, particularly gay and lesbian Catholics, scandalized again by the church's doctrine. Yet, as Alison (2021) argued in response to the CDF, we might do well to recognize it as the church having a tantrum, offering circular logic that refuses the potential for dialog on morality. The church's stance on LGBTQ issues illustrates a form of "tantrum teaching" about upholding a morality that bears little resemblance to the reality of creation. As he argued,

> where frightened morality tries to close things down, wisdom, start-
> ing from our rejects, opens up the reality of what is, as we undergo
> being forgiven for our narrow goodness and hard-heartedness, sifting
> through our fears and delusions. And so we discover our neighbours
> as ourselves, and how we are loved. (para. 9)

There is, within all this, a potential weakening of the harsh languages of prophetic indictment and the scandals it creates. This weakening, we want to suggest, points us toward the potential of weakness. There may be, as such, value in embracing weakness in our thinking so as not to lord being right over others but as a way to be with others in the work of finding what's right in context.

Rather than asserting moral righteousness and strong condemnations, which have produced cruel material consequences, we find weakness a viable stance toward alternative perceptions that do justice to the complexities while not flattening them. This, we want to suggest, can be generative for teacher educators as we grapple with student teachers in our classrooms. How can we refuse prophetic indictment, which may make us feel strong and/or good, to maintain a space in the work of education to challenge staid perceptions while cultivating new ones?

Of Weakness and Failure

Stephanie Shelton (2015) writes of the particular contextual complications that emerge for beginning teachers in the southern United States—in areas colloquially referred to as the Bible Belt—as they navigate how and in what ways they might begin to establish anti-homophobic practices in classrooms as student teachers (where they often control very little about the tone set by the mentor teacher) and, later, as teachers. What becomes clear in the data are the ways in which compromises, led by contextual factors, inevitably inflect on teacher practice as professionals navigate the difficulty of administrative, institutional, and social (religious, often) norms. Whitlock (2010), writing in a similar context in rural Georgia, narrates an experience in a teacher education course during which a student asserts of his experience as a teacher candidate,

> Dr. Whitlock, the guys in my class are bigger than I am. Some of them play football, and a few have done time. It's impossible to cover Thoreau with them. And yeah, they call each other and other people fag all the time. I hear them make gay jokes. They don't try to keep it quiet, but I can't call them on this. To start with they wouldn't pay me any attention, and then they wouldn't cooperate and let me teach. (p. 92)

Others in the class try to convince the student teacher of his obligation to stand up to these students, but Whitlock writes of his look of sad resignation as the discussion continues. A critical reader might wonder what it is, exactly, that the student wants to be "let" to teach, but the author doesn't pursue this line of questioning. She just doesn't see him "standing up" to the students in ways that are traditionally understood as supporting LGBTQ+ students and colleagues. A third study of note, from Blackburn (2014), catalogs the "activist" journey of a mid-career teacher from self-described "radical" out lesbian, to "butch dyke," "trans butch," "gender queer" (all in college), and then to "queer trans man" who is not "out" as trans in his teaching context. The challenge of the article lies in the way, when Kevin teaches it in a graduate seminar on queer theory, students often read the text and want "Jared," the subject of the piece, to advocate for his students in the ways in which he engaged politically earlier in his life and career. That is, Jared's move toward a kind of passive activism of presence, in which his gender is no longer in flux, for an outside audience of graduate students in a queer theory course is taken as a betrayal of the role a gay and/or trans activist teacher should play in schools.

A suggestion, which carries through a certain kind of reading of all three articles, is that there are correct ways to meet oppression in educational spaces, and they must be, in essence, sufficiently adversarial in their manifestations. What the research is suggesting, however, is a nuance and a focus on "ends" as well as context. It is a move to the side of confrontation that does not solve anything but that allows for different kinds of possibility. This different kind of possibility is not splashy nor confrontational, instead recognizing that, within education, the space and time for learning are more complicated. Strong responses, while often viscerally more appealing as readers, often in contexts, flare out quickly as they miss the complications and complexities in play when people meet and when people meet in the midst of becoming subjects. These are, by our lights, weak responses worthy of theorizing.

Halberstam (2011) has written about the queer possibility in emerging from failure through low theory, whereby "under certain circumstances failing . . . may offer more creative, more cooperative, more surprising ways of being in the world" (pp. 2–3). In the preceding examples, individual student teachers or teachers have failed in their interventions in ways that are fairly easy to catalog: One fails to perpetuate their own earlier sense of what teacher advocacy for LGBTQ+ students might look like; another fails to stand up, directly, to homophobic language and bullying in his classroom; another fails to symbolize activism in "acceptable" ways to a certain audience. And, certainly, there are problems that emerge from each of these situations, most especially in the second example in which students fail to be protected from certain kinds of violent language. But our suggestion here is that in the failures chronicled earlier, different possibilities emerge; direct confrontation has been elided in each of these three situations, and while direct confrontation can be a useful tool in combating homophobia (indeed it's a necessary one), it is an inherently limited one. Not every situation requires a hammer in the construction of a different schoolhouse that seeks to think seriously about the aporia of hospitality that Gilbert (2014) asks us to consider: What must we do to cultivate "theories of sexuality and education that engage the messy, ambivalent, and deeply contradictory spaces and relations of the school?" (p. xiii) Or, usefully, "one can be politically correct but conceptually flawed" (p. xiii); there are easy ways to condemn the lack of fortitude of those who fail to advocate for students in ways, from afar, that we see as preferable. But that failure, conceptually, is useful and perhaps functions as a different form of advocacy yet to be cognized. In the weakness of response here, something new becomes possible. It might, in fact, be as problematic as Kevin's queer theory students suggest, but it also might not be. So how could we think with it—it being weakness, yes, but also failure as both are so frequently wedded?

David Blumenthal (1993) wonders prominently in his book *Facing the Abusing God* "how one can speak responsibly of God and the Holocaust without excluding God's action from that event" (p. xvii). This is a form of theodicy—why, in a world with a god that is infinite and just, do bad things happen to good people?—which takes as its initial task the removal of God from the realm of the infinite and omnipotent, certainly from the just in all cases. Religious individuals believe that God was present in the Holocaust and in, as Blumenthal chooses to address, subsequent child abuse crises in religious faiths, as a powerful but imperfect figure (p. 16), which means "to have faith in a post-holocaust world is, first, to know—to recognize and to admit—that God is an abusing God, but not always" (p. 248). This personalist approach to God does a number of things, the most prominent of which helps us understand the ways in which Caputo's (2006) sense of the weakness of god might emerge from the fact that "God is the source of good and its warrant" but not "the power supply for everything that happens" (p. 73). If God is, in fact, powerful but flawed and not *all-powerful*, then human action matters precisely because it supplies directionality to the possibility for good in the world. This means, as well, that there is room not only to rage at an abusive god for their failures but also to remake the source of that good in ways that provide newness in a changing world, one in which an openness to queer possibility might, in fact, be said to emerge very clearly from or perhaps, more accurately, along with a weak god that brings the good to us out of which we might craft new becomings. This is, in a sense, one of the promises of queer theory: to recognize the inevitable new beginnings that come as new generations take on identities in changed contexts. Queer, here, is forever new while simultaneously being rooted in an ongoing history.

We are borrowing heavily from work by Gert Biesta, whose prologue in *The Beautiful Risk of Education* (2014) pulls from Caputo and is aptly titled "On the Weakness of Education." Because "education always involves a *risk*" (p. 1, emphasis in original), the most vital of which is that it will inevitably fall short of its ideals, then beginning with a model that assumes strength seeds catastrophe into the project. We can see this in various positivist approaches to schooling, most recently in the United States and elsewhere in the assumptive totality of the standards movement. If we just input the correct, scientifically based research into classrooms, as applied to students through standardized best practices, then education will no longer face the risk of failure but, instead, can assist in being an educational powerhouse. Or, that failure, when it inevitably comes, can be blamed on insufficient fidelity to the riskless application of curricula that have been perfected in the pursuit of student learning, effectively teacher-proofed along the way.

A weak education, for Biesta (2014), by contrast, allows first and foremost for creativity, which, he suggests, emerges from his sense that "education" is "an act of creation" (p. 11). It's here that he turns to Caputo's notion of weak creation, as read through the two Genesis creation myths from the Hebrew scriptures. We need not flog Biesta's work too extensively here for what we might glean— read the book; it's wonderful—but suffice to say, there is a difference for the philosopher in creating ex nihilo (from nothing) and bringing a being that already exists "into life" (p. 13). His argument is that what God does in this latter approach, from the Elohist writer, is akin to understandings of subjectivity that emerge in poststructural theories in education: Teachers are constantly engaged with beings coming into presence. They are not, to be perhaps a mite too glib, animating lumps of clay, scribing with chalk on all those blank slates, pouring into empty vessels. The real work is figuring out how to conceptualize education as working with individuals' subjectivities as they pursue life. Such educational work is to say, simply, as Alison (2003) suggests, "I'm curious to accompany you" (p. 111). To accompany students as teachers is a return, perhaps, to thinking of the journey of the curriculum long ago conceptualized by Dewey (1902). The curriculum is the map with which pedagogue and student plot their adventure.

The question, for our purposes, is, What does this work with a theology of weakness have to do with queer theory, queer studies, or, more to the point, queer bodies in (and as the subject of and being subjected to) teacher education? The first response is easy and is answered, at least partially, by a focus on subjectivities rather than fixed identity, but of course, there's more we can think with. But to the question of the violence of religion, and schools-as-religious-places aimed toward LGBTQ+ individuals, we might first return to Blumenthal (1993): a weak god, being present amid the structural, metaphysical, and literal violence perpetuated against gay and trans people is still present and, still, an abusing god. And so "protest is a religiously proper faith stance toward God" (p. 253), just as "distrust is a proper religious affection" as is "sustained suspicion" (p. 257). To think possibility in relation to religious and queer discourses isn't to dismiss the role of God in abuse; rather, it is to take the tools of critical analysis and utilize them in understanding not that God created the abuse that happened but what God's role (or, in our case, theology's role) might be in helping beings differently come into presence in education. Or we could read religion in a strong sense, as the creator of oppression and violence, or we could read religion in a weak sense, as coadjutor to oppression and violence that might also do different things. As such, we see a through line, for instance, running from the die-in at St. Patrick's in 1989 to protest the Catholic Church and Cardinal O'Connor's public dehumanization of AIDS patients and demonization of gays to, with all due humility, our interventions here. For what, by facile understandings of power, in the face of strength, is weaker than voluntary death, even symbolically? This engagement, in protest, with a failure of life calls attention, of course, to the church's purposeful damage in the world and indeed in the lives of not only gay men but also other queers, most especially during the AIDS epidemic. But suggesting that God was absent in this protest or that the die-in was a rebuttal to religion and faith misses, for instance, a much more ambivalent engagement at the level of gay individuals who not only participated but also found ways to remain in the church (O'Loughlin, 2019). Indeed, what are we to do with the fact that the first meeting of Gay Men's Health Crisis, the first documented public education meeting in answer to the AIDS crisis was held in the Church of St. Joseph in Greenwich Village in New York City? Or that the first dedicated AIDS ward was created at St. Vincent Hospital, in concert with the Sisters of Charity? Or that Pat Buckley, wife of the execrable William F. Buckley, provided significant funding for the effort? The answer is, well, we don't quite know. If we were interested in the strong version of engagement, then we might be tempted to put the damage and the service of religious denominations and their attendant theologies on a scale and seek to measure the harm against the benefit. But a weak theological engagement seeks something different: to think with the impossible.

For Caputo (2006), "the name of God is the name of an unconditional promise, not of an unlimited power. A promise made without an army to enforce it, without the sovereign power to coerce it" (p. 90). This, he asserts, is the "weak force of God. That force is the power of powerlessness" (p. 90). We make sense of this weak force by "replacing the logic of omnipotence" much in the vein of Blumenthal (1993), earlier, "with a poetics of the impossible" (p. 103). Poetics is important here, for our understanding of how to move forward thinking about the weak force particularly because, in contrast to a logic of impossibility in which the impossible cannot be, "a poetics of *the* impossible . . . hail[s] an event that is otherwise than being" (Blumenthal, 1993, p. 104). What is more powerless than dying, even if symbolically, at the feet of those you wish to protest? Why engage in this manner if we aren't thinking about the kind of unlimited promise that might come from a change of course in the face of such weakness? What, more globally, do we lose in our understanding of the world and in the ways in which we might argue for a different one if we fail to find meaning through alternative poetics rather than in the logic solely of confrontation and denunciation that requires the symbolic strength of an army of, perhaps, tweeting followers to support its weight? What might we do, in other words, with the theology of Jesus's voluntary assumption of a weak human form and his submission to a vicious death at the hands of Rome?

Elizabeth Johnson (2011), a feminist Catholic theologian—oft sanctioned by the institutional church for her work, which, we think, recommends her all the more—writes of the mystery of God in a different way that might be useful here. She notes that in a properly understood theology of God, "God is present where life is lived bravely, eagerly, responsibly, even without any explicit reference to religion" (p. 45). She expands, asserting that "the point is this: people who courageously accept themselves, who accept their own life with all its quirks and beauty and agony, in point of fact, accept holy mystery, who abides within them addressing them as self-offering love" (p. 44). This argument from immanence has a bit of a Dan Brown feel to it (Jesus was inside us all, all the time, ta-da!), but Johnson means it and comes with receipts in the form of the impossibility of understanding a concept of God with language because of the limitations that are inherent in any finite symbolic system. She suggests that any definition or explanation of God is always really just "naming toward God" (p. 20) because part of faith is not really knowing anyways, and because any being who is, in its fullness, beyond our comprehension can only partly be accounted for. We're all, when we do this, just naming whatever part of the elephant we have our hands on at the moment in the dark. But, for teacher education, this matters in part because so many of our students come to us with religious understandings of the world and what it means to teach; giving them permission to understand their religion as both worth engaging and incomplete allows for a weak stance in situations regarding students who challenge their faith. This is, as well, not unique to religious students but parallels the work that LGBTQ+ students encounter as they come into queer identity. Both moments, which we do not equate as the same but, rather, as running on parallel tracks, take on significant work as one works to distinguish the self not only from others but also from a former self. There is, we suspect, a need for grace here, remembering that for students amid becoming teachers, there is always more than meets the eye.

Faith is not knowing rather than knowing; being sure of an action isn't faith. The point here isn't to convert teacher education or queer studies to tributaries of religious studies. Rather, it is to suggest that particularly in relation to the ways in which public education is still (and will to a degree always be) religious, religious understandings of the world offer us a poetics of engagement that allows for the impossible to happen: coming to understand education as an act toward something rather than as a practice with predetermined ends. We think this matters, actually, in relation to multiculturalism as it is currently enacted in the curriculum in teacher education where, it should be said, it always fails in its goals. This is because of, of course, entrenched and structural racism, sexism, and heterosexism, among many other violent isms, persist. The problem, however, is that multiculturalism as we see it played out in the curriculum engages not only in the logic of identity but also in a strong rebuttal to the presence of oppression. There is no poetics of the impossibility here that might help us think with, for instance, our religious students, using religion itself as the curriculum and guiding them through the mapped terrain *in the direction of* something different. To suggest that we might convert them to something else through our pedagogy is and will always be logically impossible and thus will fail. And that failure will be read as a reason to (a) root out the practice of even trying and (b) as the need to do more of the same thing, more fervently. Without a proper understanding of the possibility in weakness and failure, we actually undermine our own project in the pursuit of a strength that disserves us and our students.

Endnotes

1 Somewhat rare, a diocesan theologian is hired by an individual diocese to provide
   theological guidance for the clergy and lay members of the Catholic Church in the
   area. A diocese may be as large as, for instance, a major city (in which case it may
   be called an archdiocese as in the case of Chicago) or may encompass an entire
   state as with the diocese of Charleston in South Carolina.

References

Alison, J. (2001). *Faith beyond resentment: Fragments Catholic and gay.* Herder &
      Herder.

Alison, J. (2003). *On being liked.* Herder & Herder.

Alison, J. (2005, September 27). *Collapsing the closet in the house of god* [Transcript].
      http://jamesalison.com/collapsing-the-closet-in-the-house-of-god/

Alison, J. (2021, March 22). Same sex blessings and the CDF—How to recognize
      a tantrum. *The Tablet.* https://www.thetablet.co.uk/blogs/1/1750/same-sex-
      blessings-and-the-cdf-how-to-recognise-a-tantrum

Biesta, G. J. J. (2014). *The beautiful risk of education.* Paradigm.

Blackburn, M. (2014). (Re)writing one's self as an activist across schools and sexual
      and gender identities: An investigation of the limits of LGBT-inclusive and
      queering discourses. *Journal of Language & Literacy Education, 10*(1), 1–13.

Blumenthal, D. R. (1993). *Facing the abusing god: A theology of protest.* John Knox Press.

Caputo, J. D. (2006). *The weakness of God: A theology of the event.* Indiana University
      Press

Dewey, J. (1902). *The child and the curriculum.* The University of Chicago Press.

Finkelstein, A. (2018). *After silence: A history of AIDS through its images.* University of
      California Press.

Foucault, M. (2008). *The government of self and others: Lectures at the College de France,
      1982–1983* (G. Burchell, Trans.). Palgrave Macmillan.

Foucault, M. (2014). *Wrong-doing, truth-telling: The function of avowal in justice* (S. W.
      Sawyer, Trans.; F. Brion & B. E. Harcourt, Eds.). University of Chicago Press.

Gilbert, J. (2014). *Sexuality in school: The limits of education.* University of Minnesota
      Press.

Halberstam, J. (2011). *The queer art of failure.* Duke University Press.

Johnson, E. A. (2011). *Quest for the living God: mapping frontiers in the theology of God.*
      Continuum.

Jordan, M. (1998). *The invention of sodomy in Christian theology.* University of Chicago
      Press.

Kaveny, C. (2016). *Prophecy without contempt: Religious discourse in the public square.* Harvard University Press.

Kinloch, V., & Pedro, T. S. (2014). The space between listening and storying: Foundations for projects in humanization. In D. Paris & M. T. Winn (Eds.), *Humanizing research: Decolonizing qualitative inquiry with youth and communities* (pp. 21–42). Sage Publications.

Kohler, W. (2020, June 19). Founder of the Moral Majority Jerry Falwell: "AIDS is God's punishment for homosexuals." *Back to Stonewall.* http://www.back2stonewall.com/2020/06/gay-history-june-19-1983-jerry-falwell-aids-gods-punishment-homosexuals.html

Kristeva, J. (1982). *The powers of horror: An essay on abjection.* Columbia University Press.

Latour, B. (2004). Why has critique run out of steam? From matters of fact to matters of concern. *Critical Inquiry, 30*(2), 225–248.

Martel, F. (2019). *In the closet of the Vatican: Power, homosexuality, hypocrisy.* Bloomsbury.

O'Loughlin, M. (2019). Surviving the AIDS crisis as a gay Catholic (No.1) [Audio podcast episode]. In *Plague: Untold stories of AIDS and the Catholic Church.* America: The Jesuit Review. https://www.americamagazine.org/voices/plague-untold-stories-aids-catholic-church

Pascoe, C. J. (2007). *Dude, you're a fag: Masculinity and sexuality in high school.* University of California Press.

Paulikas, S. (2017, August 14). Christianity does not justify Trump's 'Fire and Fury'. *The New York Times.* https://www.nytimes.com/2017/08/14/opinion/christianity-does-not-justify-trumps-fire-and-fury.html

Peace, R. (2001). Producing lesbians: Canonical proprieties. In D. Bell, J. Binnie, R. Holliday, R. Longhurst, & R. Peace (Eds.), *Pleasure zones: Bodies, cities, spaces* (pp. 29–54). Syracuse University Press.

Petro, A. (2015). *After the wrath of God: AIDS, sexuality and American religion.* Oxford University Press.

Salzman, T., & Lawler, M. (2008). *The sexual person: Toward a renewed Catholic anthropology.* Georgetown University Press.

Schulman, S. (2012). *The gentrification of the mind: Witness to a lost imagination.* University of California Press.

Shelton, S. A. (2015). A narrative analysis of the sociocultural factors that limit a novice teacher's LGBT activism. *Teaching Education, 26*(1), 113–130.

Silin, J. (1995). *Sex, death, and the education of children: Our passion for ignorance in the age of AIDS.* Teachers College Press.

Truett, B. (2019, May 16). 'The AIDS crisis is still beginning' says artist and activist Gregg Bordowitz. *Hyperallergic.* https://hyperallergic.com/499348/gregg-bordowitz-art-institute-of-chicago/

Whitlock, U. (2006). Queerly fundamental: Christian fundamentalism, southern queerness, and curriculum studies. *Journal of Curriculum and Pedagogy, 3*(1), 165-186.

Whitlock, U. (2010). Getting queer: Teacher education, gender studies, and the cross-disciplinary quest for queer pedagogies. *Issues in Teacher Education, 19*(2), 81–104.

Yanay, N. (2013). *The ideology of hatred: The psychic power of discourse.* Fordham University Press.

CHAPTER 4

Considering Legal Landscapes

A Preliminary Conversation

Adam: I have become interested over the past few years in the law and, in particular, what seems to be an absence of thinking about the "law" or "laws" within teacher education. Education law, in my experience, seems to be a conversation limited to education administration and leadership creating an assumption that only administrators need to know and consider the rights of educational stakeholders (e.g., students, teachers, parents). Of course, as I write this, I cringe a bit because I think teacher education is already stuffed to the brim with requirements and expectations as they emerge from various arenas including state and federal policies, education research, and professional experience. This is a reason why I am drawn to the word "consider" and its different manifestations in education. I think here about the complaint often heard in teacher education that "I have to consider everything." And this is, as we will explore, quite true. Teachers often have to consider everything as they navigate the dynamics of a classroom within the larger milieu. My interest in thinking about the law is, in part, another thing to consider for not only student teachers and subsequently in-service teachers but also teacher educators who may themselves have limited knowledge on education law. There is no way around that since schools and society are constantly responding to the changing world.

However, I am at least momentarily convinced that considering the law is central to education as the law limns the scene of schooling while also illustrating the work it takes to alter that scene as well. My sense is that we often take the law or rights accorded by laws for granted when those laws protect us or when the associated rights have simply always been "present." For those for whom such experiences are not true, the struggle for laws and rights is foundational to becoming a subject. There is already, I suspect, a certain engagement with laws and rights in different forms of "civic education." But it remains the case that laws and rights bleed into all moments of education, well beyond the explicit curriculum of, for instance, social studies classrooms. Being uninformed about the law and rights of not only students but also one's self as an adult and employee can breed further conflicts and legal snafus. Given our interest in the complexities that emerge around and between religion and sexuality and gender, it seems necessary to consider not only how those discourses and practices have been impacted by litigation and judicial decisions but also how such litigation and judicial decisions help contextualize and aid our understanding of our responsibilities as educators.

Kevin: I took my first and only course on the law in my higher education master's degree program. It was titled Education Law and Public Policy; enrollment was split fairly evenly between those of us working through a degree program for staff in higher education—seeking either permanence or advancement through the assistant and associate directorships that have popped up to serve the broad administrative support (or bloat, depending on how you want to think about it) that comes with the modern university—and second and third-year law students. I found the course fascinating, not least because of the performance of the professor, who was an adjunct with the law school at my university and who lectured for the full three hours of every single class we had together. His stamina was stunning, but so was his confidence in the material presented. He knew things, it seemed, and those of us on the higher education side of the spectrum were just learning how to read legal opinions and briefs and how to write in ways deemed acceptable (even if barely so) in legal discourse. From what I recall, the law students mostly followed live baseball game feeds on their computers. I'm not sure if the law itself was old hat to them—as they were beyond their 1L trial by Socratic fire—or if *education* law itself was considered passé. That might be too harsh: they were certainly better at absorbing case law than we outsiders to the discourse.

I found the class fascinating and difficult. At that point, I'd already gotten out of teaching high school English and was on to teaching rhetoric and writing at the collegiate level. This was before a PhD in education was even on my radar, but I do think that the experience led me, in part, to our shared program at Michigan State, not least because the degree program in which we were enrolled when we met was called Curriculum, Teaching, and Educational Policy. I didn't take a single course in education law in our doctoral program, which seems silly. If that third piece of the triad means anything, it has to consider the ways in which policy flows from and informs the law. Certainly we read around the topic. But I really wasn't prepared, when I first started researching religion and American education, for the singular focus in writing in the field on the law. Here's what happened in Supreme Court cases that made various religious practices possible and impossible; here's what happened in the history of the profession that emerged from various state and federal laws; here's what's allowed of teachers and students that need not be left "at the schoolhouse doors" in other words.

Much of how we started thinking about this book emerged from the differences in our current institutions, a research one university in the Bible Belt and an art and design school in the Midwest, and our struggling to make sense of how to, well, make sense of, the various religious discourses that might be reconsidered in teacher education if we're to think hospitality anew. I'm struck by a video of a colleague who is an expert in education law and religion. He's meeting with teacher candidates at our university and as a heuristic to think about ambiguities in the law wonders how large a cross would be legal to wear around one's neck when teaching without running afoul of First Amendment principles. The answer, of course, is it depends. But the specificity of that line of questioning, along with the ambiguity of possible answers, suggests a limiting frame that necessarily emerges from legal discourse in relation to religion, education, and, for our purposes, thinking with queerness at the top of mind. The law, it seems to me, is ambivalent about the contingency of "it depends" but, to a large degree, relies on this gray area for its authority: It depends in infinite regress through case law as it builds a de facto rationale for (un)popular social understandings of the acceptable. So stare decisis is a norm until it isn't in the same way that the cross is legal until it isn't, depending on who's making the decision. We won't know the moment things cross the line (pun intended) until after the fact. There's a need, I think, to live in the future perfect, then, when we think about legal landscapes: What will have been matters a great deal more and is better to attend to than what was or what is. However, we need also to understand antecedents to imagine possible futures.

I'm not optimistic about the trajectory of legal issues in the United States regarding LGBTQ+ rights as they are positioned both in the law and in the zeitgeist contra religious freedom. The first question should always be, clearly, religious freedom for whom and to what end? But more so, even in the face of *Bostock*, we have *Trinity Lutheran v. Comer* but we also have the relatively new Religious Exemption Accountability Project, which seeks to use Title IX to challenge religious discrimination at *Christian* colleges on legal grounds. There's a push–pull here that we should help our students understand just as we try to move them beyond legal frameworks as the primary epistemological approach to religious and LGBTQ+ issues in schools.

It seems fruitful, then, to wonder together about how to consider the legal landscape both as it exists, per se, and as it exists as a framing device for consideration itself. The rhetoric around teacher education, as Adam rightly notes, sits in a space of too much: There are too many requirements to consider anything anew (or again). This is much of the argument that pushes foundations of education to the edges of the field even as it atomizes the practice of our work. I'm in English education; Adam's in art education. Neither of us is *in* the philosophy or theology of education, but of course, that's the wrong construction. The boundaries of certification never fully belie the underlying theories that make them possible, but I think, more important for our framing, impossible as well.

On Consideration

Within teacher education, there exists a sentiment, perhaps an exasperated complaint, expressed by many students that they have to "consider everything." This is, as well, a sentiment felt by teacher educators as they navigate not only the revolving door of education reform and new findings in education research but also the changing student body and their emergent ideas and needs. To consider, as its definition informs us, is to think carefully about something before making a decision. We consider things and in doing so are able to make decisions—decisions informed by our thinking. This is easier written than done given the realities that teachers—be they teacher educators, K–12 practitioners, or student teachers—have to make innumerable decisions across the span of any given day amid, quite often, challenging conditions. Although such decisions arguably do not become easier to make, experience provides us with insights and shortcuts into making them. As we consider more and more things, such considerations become part of our repertoire, allowing us to become, in time, considerate teachers. However, such experience can also thwart us from considering things anew or differently as the world turns. We can fall back on our experience and in doing so fall down on the job of considering everything. Or, as Britzman (2007) reminds us, "somehow the having of experience dulls our thinking. Somehow, the uncertainty that is our beginning has become predictable and routine" (p. 3). We can, with experience, become inconsiderate when our considerations disallow us from thinking through our decisions or when we tire of considering everything to instead rest on our experience.

Having to consider everything can, on the surface, sound overwhelming. It is, we think. Thinking about and through the various issues, stakeholders, and different learners requires skills and knowledge acquired through experience. Such experience, we want to maintain, is not limited to "being in a classroom" as a teacher but inclusive of the entirety of our experience as "students," "student teachers," and "teachers," with each "position" bringing different insights into what can be or should be considered, remembering, of course, that privileging any one position limits what considerations the others bring to a conversation. This is one reason why we see the audience for this book as inclusive of all three positions. We work from the belief that all parties would do well to think together about their immediate relations as students and teachers as they also think forward to their relations with future students or, put differently, in considering everything we need to consider the necessary work that teacher educators are always amid as they are asking student teachers to do work, and student teachers need to consider the necessary work of teacher educators instead of projecting forward to their future classroom, thus ignoring or (in many cases) hating their teacher education classes. The issues that educators—at any level—have to consider are largely quite similar, so working toward transparency in educational relations might help in the uncertain work of becoming considerate.

This becomes most visible for us when we turn to the legal landscape of education, an area of consideration rarely taken up within teacher education despite the ways in which the law immediately frames education, provides insights into the rights of teachers and students, along with their responsibilities in their roles. We might note here that this hole in teacher education very much connects to the withering on the vine of foundations of education as a field in the broader landscape of education. This, of course, has come about through the incessant credentialing first utilized by the field of teacher education to

assert itself through professionalization and then increasingly imposed exter-
nally from accrediting bodies, state legislatures, and through various federal
mandates (Burbules & Densmore, 1991; Labaree, 1997). A generalized history
of education (and its discontents) within teacher education curricula wherein
one might encounter a historicizing of the legal terrain of education is, as many
readers will know, comparatively rare now. There just isn't room in the student
requirements we tell ourselves, and although this is both true and untrue in
many ways, it is certainly becoming received wisdom across the United States.

In considering legal landscapes in this chapter, we want to scratch the surface of how court cases assist in providing educators—teacher educators and
student teachers—necessary insights into both the histories of educational
struggle and the use of such histories in understanding our contemporary landscapes. We start here by homing in on key court cases and legal decisions on
religion, sexuality, and gender. And we do so with a belief that considering legal
landscapes assists educators in larger political and ethical work.

Legal cases, at their heart, are rooted in some form of conflict. Competing
ideas about education or claims to rights come head-to-head in the courthouse
to help frame education—be it questions about curriculum (e.g., evolution vs.
creationism in *Scopes*) or student extracurricular groups (e.g., *East High Gay
Straight Alliance v. Board of Education*). While the vast majority of educators
will avoid becoming litigants in court cases, through some certain legal cases
in education, we can glimpse successes and failures in cultivating educational
relations. Such successes and failures, in a sense, fall back on our abilities to
consider "everything" and the reality that we cannot do so; our failings expose
new things we might or should consider next time.

This brings us into the realm of ethics. In Lynn Fendler's (2011) dialog
"Edwin and Phyllis," this reckoning with failure informs Phyllis, a teacher and
amateur theorist. When asked by Edwin, an aspiring teacher, what "ethical"
means to her, she responds,

> For me, personally, 'ethical' has two parts, both of which are dynamic:
>
> • Keep challenging my assumptions about what is good
> • Do less harm next time. (p. 469)

To do less harm next time centralizes the reality that harm is inevitable in education, whereby a vital task for teachers becomes repairing such harms and learning from their inevitable harmful actions for "next time." This focus on doing less harm operates alongside a related challenge to "question our assumptions about what is good." Teaching is, at its heart, relational work—something we explore in various ways throughout this book—and such work is dynamic as it navigates both how we impact others and how our knowledge is questioned. Our relations are related to knowledge and vice versa. And so the work of becoming a teacher, of being a teacher, asks us that we consider everything while questioning our assumptions about what we consider and doing such things so we might "do less harm next time." This, of course, takes time and recognizes dynamic realities in play. It is also, we suggest, tied to a certain Christian schema of intimacy rooted less in merit and more in charity. "We have blind spots," as Melissa Sanchez (2019) notes in *Queer Faith*,

> that will catch us unaware; we will make compromises that will appear as such only in retrospect. . . . In short, we are neither innocent nor invulnerable—whatever our hopes and intentions, we will inflict as well as suffer pain and disappointment. (p. 4)

This is especially true for teachers who may very well suffer from a violent sense of saviorism that thwarts them from being charitable to themselves and others.

The bare point is that we can't possibly consider everything. There's impossibility there, an aporia, like that of hospitality and forgiveness, which we explore later. In failing at omniscience teachers and teacher educators turn to experience as a proxy for considering *more*, and this experience is joyous, painful, banal, surprising, and fetishized. This means it's also useful. Such experience broadening our considerations moves us to recognize the work of ethics in teaching. Fendler's (2011) dynamic sense of ethics in teaching grounds our work as we challenge assumptions around sexualities, genders, and religion as they enter not only teacher education classrooms but also classrooms in public schools. If ethics—at its heart—is about relationality, then engaging sexuality, gender, and religion means considering seriously our assumptions about what it means not only to do good work but also to do less harm when we recognize that we have failed at goodness. Or, put differently, we do well when we question our own goodness and the systems that it can create. Such dynamic work is challenging; demanding that teachers put themselves at risk while working with students who themselves are amid what Gert Biesta (2014) called "the beautiful risk of education."

Given this, how can we envision dealing with the legal risks always already implicated in the work of education? This, particularly when we recognize that a key component of education is, as Hannah Arendt pointed out, helping students both recognize the world they were born into and did not make while helping to transform that world in new ways. We want to suggest here the necessary import of considering the legal landscapes that provide not only the backdrop for what can or cannot happen in schools but that also continue to be a key site where education's possibilities are determined. To consider legal landscapes is to think carefully about the ways school is both a space and time where subjects—students and teachers—come into their rights and up against legal conflicts. However, it is equally important to recognize that the law is a blunt instrument. The work of educators in classrooms requires an understanding of this blunt instrument so that they can do more fine-grained work as they navigate the complex and often contradictory realities in classrooms and school grounds.

A Legal Opening

For legal scholar Justin Driver (2018), "one cannot plausibly claim to understand public education in the United States today, that is, without appreciating how the Supreme Court's decisions involving students' constitutional rights shape the everyday realities of schools across the country" (p. 9). Students' constitutional rights are strangely enough rarely a topic within teacher education, burdened as the field is with an ever-changing onslaught of research, reforms, and rhetoric (Cuban, 2013; Labaree, 2010; Tyack & Cuban, 1995). Yet teachers are inevitably on the front lines of how students experience their constitutional rights, including the denial of those rights. Although we are not legal scholars, we find it necessary and important to address the legal landscape, expansively if not exhaustively, for the ways it forms and informs how teachers might enter classrooms and encounter students as emerging subjects. Teachers, as frontline workers for the education of citizens, need not be legal scholars; rather, there is a need for educators to consider the legal landscape, granted some fluency, that they might make informed decisions regarding school-based decision-making. Put differently, without considering the legal landscape, teacher educators and their student teachers are positioned to not be able to consider the ways the courts have shaped and continue to shape the ways subjects come into presence as legal, rights-bearing subjects.

Returning to Driver's insight, however, we explore the ways in which the legal landscape, notably, but not exclusive to Supreme Court decisions, is important to the work of becoming a teacher. This is not only so that teachers don't deny students their constitutional rights but also so that those rights are taken into consideration when thinking through curriculum and everyday encounters in schools. We recognize, as such, a thick conception of education and citizenship whereby schools would do well to engage students in ways that build in and on their near future as "adults." Or, put differently, we do not hold onto the idea that "children should be seen and not heard"; instead, we recognize that children should be engaged fully and educationally as they come to understand the meanings and responsibilities of "citizenship." More specific to our purposes, Kunzman (2006) argues:

> We can and should help students learn how to talk about religion and morality, learn how to discuss disagreements that are influenced by religious and other ethical perspectives—not because we can "solve" them, but because this grappling is the responsibility of informed, respectful citizenship. (p. 2)

To do this requires, we think, a rich understanding of the complicated and changing legal landscape around religious expression, sexual, and gender identity, and the rights and protections that students are provided (or aren't).

Because our concerns within this book are centered on the tensions and possibilities between "religion" and "sexuality and gender," we focus this chapter on the range of legal questions and overlaps that exist as these issues enter the school and classroom. In doing so, we want to note that there are limits to the law but that we cannot entirely recognize those limits if we don't know the law to begin with. Furthermore, we cannot do justice to the work of religion and sexuality and gender without recognizing the ways in which those "things" are framed by the law, indeed created by it in many ways. This history of legal decisions is far more complex and complicated than we are able to address in one chapter. Our intention in scratching the surface here is to open the conversation as to the necessity for considering the legal landscape as it has both framed our current educational system and will continue to frame (or reframe) that system through struggle and new considerations.

Public schools have been, as scholars and politicians have articulated, a central institution to the development and evolution of "American democracy" (Black, 2020). As such, public schools have been a key site for, as Driver (2018) argues, the battle for the American mind. And while we will engage the various battles for the American mind below, we add that such battles are also for the American body and soul. This, we sense, becomes more apparent as we address emerging legal battles over the rights of transgender students' access to school facilities from bathrooms to locker rooms. While such battles address mindsets—changing or otherwise—about the concept of gender, they also in very real ways rest on the physical bodies of students and the complex understandings of "gender" as they intersect with "biological sex." More on this later.

Whether addressing religion or sexuality and gender, it seems fair to say that the issues presented are politically fraught. This is true, quite broadly, for many issues regarding students' constitutional rights that impact the education of youth. As Driver (2018) articulates, "bringing these matters into the educational arena elevates the temperature higher still, both because the cases tend to involve minors and because of the central place that public schools occupy in the nation's cultural imagination" (p. 11). This cultural imagination is arguably never singular but complicated by the pluralistic realities of the United States and its public school population, whose demographics have shifted dramatically since its founding and remain shifting continually. After all, in 2021, on any given day, about one sixth of the American population can be found in public schools, so with such a large swathe of the population involved, it makes sense that conflicts and disputes exist.

As we jump into exploring some legal landscapes, it is important to recognize the tension that will be in play for cases addressing "religion," "sexuality and/or gender," and, of course, their overlap. The various cases that we explore illustrate tensions arguably always already present in schools. Put differently, teachers are always having to consider different stakeholders and how those stakeholders may agree or disagree around given decisions. They also have to think about themselves, as stakeholders who may themselves be implicated in debates about the right to be out. "The right to be out encompasses—but is not limited to," as Biegel (2010) argues, "disclosure of one's race, ethnicity, religion, sexual orientation, gender identity, political views, medical conditions, past experiences, present involvement, and future plans" (p. xiii). Thinking through the legal landscape and the right to be out adds an additional layer to consider, often around what these different stakeholders are allowed or not allowed to do within the space of public schools. The particular stakeholders we can see within schools are students, parents, the school, the community (including any number of religious establishments), and the government. Tensions emerge between students and schools (e.g., Can a school infringe on students' free expression?), between schools and parents (e.g., Can parents opt out of portions of a public school curriculum?), between students and parents (e.g., Can a student go against parental wishes at school?), and between students and peers (e.g., Do students have privacy rights vis-à-vis other students?). Abstractly, these can seem rather settled. And, in some sense, they are settled until they are unsettled by changing precedents and courts but, more to the point, by the bodies that enter schools. To think about and through the law—particularly as we are interested here—is to allow for a conversation about the contradictions and complexities in play within educational relations that are never merely between people but surrounded and informed by various discourses.

Religion and Its Legal Questions

Religion has consistently held a central and contested place within American public schools. There are, as we touched on earlier, histories of struggles around the place of religion be it the identity of students, the curriculum, or rituals within schools. Since the 1960s, Justice and Macleod (2016) argue, "the court ruled on a string of cases, delineating the proper relationship between religion and public schooling in all manner of detail" (p. 103). These Supreme Court decisions illustrate the Court's stance on the Establishment Clause and Free Exercise Clause regarding students in schools. These cases include *Engels v. Vitale*

(1962), which invalidated New York state's requirement that students recite the "Regent's Prayer"; *Abington School District v. Schempp* (1963), decided a year later, which invalidated state laws that required reciting the Lord's Prayer and Bible verses at the start of the school day; and *Stone v. Graham* (1980) which ruled against the display of the Ten Commandments in public schools. Each of these key decisions endowed students with "enhanced protections" at least in theory; religious actors have, however, argued vehemently that decisions restricting religious expression in schools by state actors, in fact, diminishes protections for religious individuals. The tension between the Free Exercise Clause and the Establishment Clause is meant to, at least in how it's often discussed in legal circles, maintain an uneasy balance between the rights of religious and irreligious individuals and supposed secular governmental institutions.

The court's work in the mid-20th century established precedent that sought to give balance to this tension. Indeed, this was the purpose of the creation, in 1971, of the Lemon test (from *Lemon v. Kurtzman*, 1973), which proposed a three-pronged consideration when addressing legislation concerning religion. As with any test, seeking objective measures creates as many problems as it solves, but the point is that the court attempted to hold itself accountable to balance the tensions required by the First Amendment's religion clauses. As the court has moved to the right in the last 30 years on religious freedom issues, it has also moved left on issues related to sexuality and gender. At the same time, the current court has seemed much more willing to err on the side of Free Exercise at the expense of antiestablishment jurisprudence. There will inevitably be effects on schools to these diametric shifts, as well as on teacher and student bodies in these schools. Still, history is important for understanding the ongoing shift of tectonic legal plates.

Within the *Engels* decision, the justices in the majority sought to help distinguish between the Establishment Clause and the Free Exercise Clause. Writing for the majority, Justice Hugo Black argued:

> Although these two clauses may in certain instances overlap, they forbid two quite different kinds of governmental encroachment upon religious freedom. The Establishment Clause, unlike the Free Exercise Clause, does not depend upon any showing of direct governmental compulsion and is violated by the enactment of laws which

establish an official religion whether those laws operate directly to coerce non- observing individuals or not. This is not to say, of course, that laws officially prescribing a particular form of religious worship do not involve coercion of such individuals. When the power, prestige and financial support of government is placed behind a particular religious belief, the indirect coercive pressure upon religious minorities to conform to the prevailing officially approved religion is plain. (pp. 430–431)

The state has to avoid establishing or prescribing any particular form of religious worship—hence invalidating the practice of required prayer in school as well as the reading of Bible verses except in such courses as those that treat the Bible as a form of literature, among many others. Yet, at the same time, the state cannot stop students from expressing their religious beliefs, making sure that students do not have to shed their religious identity at the school's doorsteps.

Decisions addressing the concerns about the Establishment Clause starting with the *Engel* decision and moving forward "demonstrate," as Driver (2018) maintains,

> awareness both that the public school setting potentially imposes acute coercive pressure on students' beliefs and that this religiously diverse nation must take special steps to forestall any notion that simply receiving an education subjects students to proselytization. (pp. 362–363)

Put differently, the court has consistently recognized that coercion is particularly concerning within schools given their compulsory nature and the religious diversity of the United States. As such, there need to be particular steps to ensure students receive an education as relatively free from religious proselytization as can be in a historically and culturally Christian society.

Students, as a result of these key decisions, cannot, legally, be coerced into involuntarily participating in religious observance. However, these decisions do not, as just noted, require students to shed their religious identity at the schoolhouse doors. This is perhaps most visible with the Supreme Court's decision to uphold the Equal Access Act in *Mergens v. Westside School District* (1989), which allowed students to initiate extracurricular groups of a religious nature. The Equal Access Act, passed in 1984 by Congress and signed into law by Ronald Reagan, required that students have equal access to extracurricular clubs in public secondary schools. As Secretary of Education Arne Duncan noted in a 2011 letter addressing LGBTQ+ bullying and harassment in schools, the Equal Access Act was "rooted in principles of equal treatment and freedom of expression" that sought to "protect[ ] student-initiated groups of all types" (Duncan, 2011, para. 4). "By allowing students to discuss difficult issues openly and honestly, in a civil manner," Duncan maintains, "our schools become forums for combating ignorance, bigotry, hatred, and discrimination" (2011, para. 4). In an ironic twist, the fight for students' rights to extracurricular religious groups paved the way for the rights of LGBTQ+ students to form groups as well. Ronald Reagan, in a deliciously perverse sense, becomes the father of Gay-Straight Alliances (GSAs), with an act he signed upholding the rights of students to initiate extracurricular groups addressing issues of sexuality and gender.

These Supreme Court decisions, importantly, do not preclude teachers from addressing the role of religion in society as part of their responsibilities as pedagogues. Rather, they prohibit teachers from leading pupils in religious exercises and protect students from coerced participation in such exercises. These trends over the past 60-odd years have, as Driver (2018) argues, "had the salutary consequence of diminishing the erroneous notion that religion and education must remain wholly separate" (p. 398). We are, ourselves, wont to agree with Driver's assessment, at least on the legal level. However, we are unsure if the erroneous notion that religion and education must remain wholly separate has diminished as much on the ground of teacher education where students continue to question and express a diverse range of ideas about the role of religion, if any, within public schools. The notion of "separation" remains quite present despite the fact that, as Driver points out,

> the more useful Establishment Clause test turns not on strict separation but on neutrality, inquiring whether the state's conduct through its express terms either advances or inhibits religion and non-religion. (p. 414)

There is, within the language used to engage the Establishment Clause, a need to move away from strict "separation" toward neutrality that neither promotes nor denies religion. This move toward neutrality can be seen within the Supreme Court's decisions. The court's decisions in the 1960s and 1970s were, as Justice and Macleod (2016) illustrated, indicative of strict separationist arguments. However, starting in the 1990s and 2000s, the court shifted in cases around homeschooling and vouchers to take a more accommodationist approach. Such cases (e.g., *Wisconsin v. Yoder*, 1972, on homeschooling; *Zelman v. Simmons-Harris*, 2002, on vouchers for religious schools), though complicated, illuminate how the court has both established separation and accommodation depending on a range of issues. This doctrine of (roughly) equal application, whereby public accommodations for religion had to match accommodations for other, secular groups, has shifted significantly in recent shadow docket cases decided by the Roberts court in the face of COVID-19 public health provisions. It appears that we may be reentering an era of historic preference for religious expression in the law (Liptak, 2021). This will no doubt have significant effects on schools, teachers, and students.

Taken together, however, as the law, as a blunt instrument, enters localities and is put to work (or ignored), we might find ourselves able to see, as Labaree (2010) argues, the beauty of public education's ability to withstand reforms. School prayer and scripture reading are less a "thing" in public education, and the dreams of privatizing public education through vouchers and homeschooling remain marginal, if latent. Noting this, of course, is not to suggest we should not be vigilant. Rather, it is to suggest that we consider the range of cases that have been decided and what they allow us to think about across the complex terrain of public education. This also, we think, asks that within the educational relations of teacher education we think like educators, which is to say as weak, rather than strong, activists to address the complexity of the issues involved. These issues may seem resolved or morally central from our vantage point as teacher educators but a key component of teaching is helping bring our students, who will be teachers, into these conversations and the array of viable approaches and viewpoints that coexist within the fraught democratic project.

There are, after all, always grey areas in education. This is why we have to, as educators, consider everything and be open to those moments when our considerations fail. What the legal landscape reveals to us is a range of tensions that emerge. These tensions can, from a certain kind of activist viewpoint, be positioned as cut and dry. Yet, within educational relations, tensions are the very stuff of cultivating ethical positions and engaging in an educational project as students come into understanding and being. What we mean here is that there needs to be a way in which the uncertainties of education and learning are allowed to be traveled through in teacher education and engaged in, in a way that strong "activist" discourses can shut down in favor of certainty. This is not, however, to advocate that activist discourses should themselves be shut out, but rather recognized as one form of discourse within educational relations.

A tension here is visible within a history of legal challenges rooted in definitions of religious freedom. For instance, as Justice and Macleod (2016) illustrate, evangelical Christians, in response to the decisions in the 1960s and 1970s that showed a separationist approach by the court, "adopted the language of the civil rights movement to claim that they were victims of discrimination" (pp. 106–107). This adopted language helped sway the courts to take a more accommodationist stance (alongside, the changing court itself). This claim, as well, is a central issue of concern here as we consider the ways competing stances on discrimination come in contact. And while the courts help decide the veracity of such claims, the claims themselves impact the classroom environment in ways that exceed legal logics. Before getting ahead of ourselves, however, let us shift gears to think through the emerging legal landscapes around sexuality and gender identity.

Queer Legal Landscapes

Religion and religious liberty have been front and center in the stories that get told about U.S. history and citizenship, particularly given the reality that the United States is a uniquely religiously diverse nation. However, by the late 20th century and into the 21st century, additional challenges based on citizenship emerged within schools. As Justice Brennan noted in *Plyler v. Doe* (1982), which argued that states do not have the right to deny public education from students based on immigration status, "education is necessary to prepare citizens to participate effectively in our open political system if we are to preserve freedom and independence" (p. 457). Schools, as a context of central importance to citizenship, continue to navigate a range of complex issues centered on sexual orientation and gender identity, drawing on at least 50 years of emerging case law, addressing, quite broadly, the right to be out as an LGBTQ+ citizen. This includes moves to require sensitivity training and improve antidiscrimination policies. Yet, as Marquez and Brockenbrough (2013) point out,

> if court victories against homophobic discrimination continue to compel school districts to respond with revised antidiscrimination policies and mandatory sensitivity trainings, how can we be sure that such measures will benefit all queer students if the differential impact of multiple oppressions is not taken into account (p. 470)

We probably cannot be sure of the benefits of such reforms, in part, since our knowledge of the law is quite limited and changing. Additionally, school, like organized religion, sports, and the military, continues to be an institution that struggles with the stigmatization of homosexuality and gender nonconformity, particularly as it intersects with race. As Marquez and Brockenbrough argue, "it is important to ask questions about the intersections of identities and power that seem to have been overlooked in legal discourses of queer students' rights" (2013, p. 476). These demographic changes emerging amid a range of liberation struggles, including gay liberation and gay rights movements, centered new issues in schools that altered the duties, responsibilities, and rights of those involved, be they students, teachers, or administrators.

Amid demographic changes and the emergence of new cultural communities, the law had to—alongside other institutions—respond to changing demands and calls for protection. The legacies of these struggles, key to the promises of liberalism, are themselves rooted in the ways religious diversity had been fought for in affirming not only ideas of religious liberty and diversity but also protecting such ideas from state overreach. How does the state maintain religious liberty and neutrality while also protecting ideas, practices, and communities that may be at odds with the beliefs of any given religion? A simple answer is that it does so in a range of ways with mixed results and continued uncertainty. While we might hope the law provides us with answers—certain answers—we would do better to recognize that the law provides us with grey areas within which we must operate. Fortunately, the Supreme Court's 2020

decision in *Bostock v. Clayton County Georgia* did prohibit employment discrimination based on sexual orientation or gender identity, clarifying the meaning
of "because of . . . sex" stated in Title VII of the Civil Rights Act. This decision,
however, did not address other forms of discrimination within housing and
healthcare. Its impact on education via Title IX will be seen in the coming years
and decades. However, as the National School Board Association (2020) notes,
"because the Court decided that the federal law protects employees from being
fired due to their status as gay or transgender, that federal protection now exists
in every state" (p. 7). This is basic protection against being fired based on one's
gay or transgender status, although many states have their own human rights
protections. As such, it remains the case that when it comes to the rights of
LGBTQ+ persons, such gains have expanded to the federal level regarding employment but remain dependent on location and region in other regards (e.g.,
dress codes, bathroom access, locker room access). There remain, however,
religious carve-outs to these protections that allow parochial schools to fire
teachers for being gay or trans (Riley, 2020) and to discriminate against queer
students even in publicly funded religious schools (see Maxwell, 2021). Many
of these moves rely on broad readings of the so-called ministerial exemption
which bars the application of antidiscrimination laws in the case of "ministers"
of a given denomination. The ambiguity about who counts as a minister feeds
uncertainty but has been read to include teachers employed by religious schools
who are otherwise uninvolved in specific religious instruction.

It is important to recognize, as Stuart Biegel (2010) notes, "the duty to
supervise on school grounds under tort law is generally viewed as a duty to
protect students, not as a duty to protect teachers" (p. 71). This causes a wrinkle
in teacher education given the realities, more and more, that students becoming teachers were very likely educated in contexts that provided them an array
of protections and access to, for instance, GSAs. These protections include
not only protections from bullying and harassment but also rights to be out
as LGBTQ+ students. From the *Nabozny* decision in 1996 that made school
districts liable for failing to protect students based on sexual orientation to
cases affirming the rights of GSAs to exist on K–12 campuses (e.g., *Colin v.
Orange Unified School District*, 2000), LGBTQ+ students have, broadly if in-
completely, garnered protections and the right to be out at least in a legal sense.
These twinned realities illustrate the intimate connection between the First

Amendment's Free Expression clause and the Fourteenth Amendment's Equal Protection clause, a connection often affirmed in cases involving LGBTQ+ student rights.

As students in teacher education, however, the challenge becomes one of shifting from recognizing the rights and protections of LGBTQ+ students and the potential limitations or risks currently implicated in being an LGBTQ+ teacher. All is not lost, of course, as LGBTQ+ teachers have an array of protections and rights to be out. As Biegel (2010) put it, "although public school educators cannot feel as free as their students might feel to speak about their lives, identities, and personal perspectives, neither must they feel they have to keep their identities to themselves" (p. 49). This reality was affirmed, as noted earlier with the *Bostock* decision, although given the newness of the decision its use within public education has yet to be seen. Nonetheless, it offers gay and transgender teachers in public schools basic federal employment protections against being fired for their gay or transgender identities.

Beyond these basic federal employment protections, however, teachers' rights to be out vary by jurisdiction. This means, as Biegel (2010) notes, "LGBT educators face more covert pressures [than LGBT students], and they are often confronted with the message that they had better remain as closeted as possible" (p. xvii). Remaining closeted may be waning in some areas, but the legacies of homophobia and transphobia remain within schools as conspiracy fears of "queer recruitment" persist (Rosky, 2013). Additionally, research shows that adults within K–12 school settings continue to not only look the other way but also participate in the mistreatment and harassment of both LGBTQ+ students and teachers (Kosciw et al., 2018). This reality confirms what Antonin Scalia argued in his dissenting opinion in the Supreme Court's 2003 decision *Lawrence v. Texas*: "many Americans do not want persons who openly engage in homosexual conduct . . . as scoutmasters for their children, [or] as teachers in their children's schools" (p. 602) Scalia's opinion was in the minority as antisodomy laws were struck down, but his sentiment operates with a presumption of majority favor. This is the danger lurking in a pluralistic society.

There have yet to be, as of this writing, any education cases engaging LGBTQ+ status at the U.S. Supreme Court. Gavin Grimm's case against Gloucester County School Board had reached the Supreme Court but was vacated in 2017 with a change in policy after the election of Donald Trump. It was remanded to the lower courts. In August 2020, the Fourth Circuit Court decided in favor of Gavin Grimm, relying heavily on their interpretation of the *Bostock* decision. In February 2021, the Gloucester County School Board submitted a writ of certiorari to the Supreme Court to have the decision of the Fourth Circuit reviewed. The Supreme Court, in the end, declined to hear the appeal, allowing the Fourth Circuit's decision to stand. As such, most decisions and gains that have been made for LGBTQ+ teachers have been in lower state and federal courts. This continues the reality that the right to be out for teachers varies, requiring teachers (and, we argue, student teachers) to be attentive to the local policies and protections provided by district and state laws (Greteman, 2019). "Public school educators may have an emerging right to be out under the law," as Biegel (2010) affirms, "but in day-to-day educational practice—and particularly in certain communities—that right may be severely curtailed" (p. 49). The curtailment of the right to be out—an "expressive identity right"—will continue to be litigated and challenged in the coming years, including looking at state and district-level codes that often include a vague statement of dismissal based on immoral or unprofessional conduct.

While religion and LGBTQ+ issues are often hot-button, fraught topics, the reality is far more nuanced due to the diverse ways some religious communities and belief systems affirm LGBTQ+ people and the fact that LGBTQ+ people are often active in various religions. These everyday realities might be rather important within schools and teacher education. The tensions so often held up between religious and progressive sexual and gender discourses ought not be seen as the sole way in which these discourses interact. Other viewpoints exist that we would do well to draw on and build from. For Biegel (2010), the "extensive dialogue, especially within various subgroups of organized religion, has led many to conclude this area is highly nuanced and that it merits careful and multi-faceted exploration over time" (p. 17). Education, as we believe throughout this book, does its best with nuanced and multifaceted explorations that rest on the complexities and uncertainties that are implicit when people meet in the world. The legal landscapes—just glimpsed earlier—illustrate parallel struggles within schools for the promises of democracy in education as students and teachers make sense of their roles and responsibilities with one another. These promises are not so much principled but rather, as Koppelman (2020) argues, "to accurately discern the interests at stake and cobble together an approach that gives some weight to each of those interests" (p. 4). For teacher educators and student teachers the task here becomes one of recognizing the shifting legal realities that come with transitioning from "student" to "teacher." These shifting realities ask that we think not only through legal landscapes but also the material consequences of such shifts on the lives of student teachers.

Considering Everything in Teacher Education

We cannot, to be clear, consider everything all at once as teachers, particularly within the shifting landscape of the law, not to mention the parsing of terms within legal discourses. Nor do we know everything we have to consider until such things are brought to our attention when tensions arise within relations. But we have to attempt to consider everything as we look across a sea of faces, interpret student reactions, and respond to the myriad things in play, at any given moment, in a classroom. For student teachers, such a sentiment emerges over time as they are asked to think about a range of issues, histories, practices, and educational research. What they are asked to consider depends on the context of their teacher education program—be it more focused on technical components (e.g., writing objectives, behavioral management), practical components (e.g., curriculum and instruction), or conceptual components (e.g., philosophies and theories). And even within these diverse components, how students are allowed or asked to consider their relation to "teaching and learning" varies. However, what might be common is that student teachers while in teacher education become experts in lack, able to point out what is lacking in their education, which, as Britzman (2007) notes, may have to do with being defensive toward the uncertainties that are part of becoming and being a teacher. Our sense, given this reality, is that amid the diversity of teacher education programs, each of these components surfaces, just in different ways framed through different politics, ideologies, and communities. Teaching requires teachers to consider a range of issues that are refracted through curricular choices, instructional strategies, conflict resolution, and so much more to assist in the process of their students' learning. Yet no matter the choices of teacher educators, there are going to be whole areas left unconsidered because of time and the ways becoming a teacher unfolds. These untouched areas emerge in moments that remind teachers of the dynamic and fraught work of teaching and learning.

For Sharon Feiman-Nemser (2012), it is useful to help students—particularly student teachers—to understand that becoming a teacher is a long-term process with little certainty. We can never learn to consider everything within our teacher education programs. Rather, for Feiman-Nemser, it is a process that can be broadly broken down into four steps—from our 12 to 16 years as students, or what she calls our pretraining phase, during which we develop all kinds of ideas about "teaching" to our time in a teacher education program; the preservice phase, during which we begin to encounter the complexities of teaching—having, we might say, the curtain pulled back to show that the all-mighty wizard (teacher) is but a person. Upon graduation, teachers embark on the in-service phase—that can be divided between the first year of teaching where the rubber meets the road for the first time as the hyphen falls away and student teachers become "teachers" in their own classroom and subsequent years where a certain level of mastery emerges with in-service teaching fostering a persona, curricula, and more.

Unique to teacher education, such research illustrated, is the reality that teachers entering classrooms existed within similar classrooms themselves, often only a few short years prior, as students. It is a profession—unlike law or medicine—in which one spends one's formative years watching teachers through an "apprenticeship of observation" (Lortie, 1975). One of the characteristics of this experience in schools is that what teacher education students "learned as students" though it impacts "what they might teach students" has "little relevancy for *how* or *who* they might be teaching" (Segall, 2002, p. 133). Teaching, from a student's perspective, can look easy since a student is rarely if ever allowed to see the work teachers do "behind the scenes" to prepare lessons and be a part of the school's larger sociocultural environment, not to mention holding space for the diverse students within their purview. As students, we are not tasked with considering the background work teachers do to create space and time for our own learning and the learning of our peers. Additionally, a key hope within teaching is that one's students become knowledgeable and skillful subjects. This means for teachers, as professionals, one does not seek to maintain one's "superior" status. Rather, one hopes to create educational spaces and opportunities for students to grow into unique selves that can and/or will enter the world to do various things (including, perhaps, return to the classroom as teachers). While this requires in our estimation that teachers be incredibly smart, a teacher's "smarts" are for the purpose of educating young people to become smart themselves, particularly regarding how everyday decisions may be implicated in an array of legal questions. The relationship to "smarts" is not one meant to maintain a hierarchy but to aid new individuals in becoming a part of the teaching world both to understand that world and be able to transform it.

It is difficult, however, for teachers in our current contexts and conditions to get smart on everything that is needed to cultivate and create those "educative" spaces and experiences. This is due to the diverse ways in which "teacher preparation" exists—from traditional teacher education programs (which are our interest) and alternative routes to certification/licensure (like Teach For America). Each approach and, as such, each program frames the work of teaching and learning in different ways ensuring that in K–12 schools, there will be a plethora of approaches to consider among one's colleagues. Teaching lies beyond a focus on preparation, a profession whose history is fraught. This fraught history is due to various factors including the realities of it being a "feminized" profession and therefore battling against legacies of sexism and misogyny alongside the ways teaching, unlike other professions, engages a clientele (e.g., students) that is both captive and often unwilling for any number of reasons. Yet teaching as a profession—despite the seemingly ever-present teacher shortages of late—appears to be experiencing a possible resurgence evidenced from the teacher strikes of the late 2010s (in primarily "red" states) and the recognition during the COVID-19 pandemic that the work of teachers is, in fact, not easy nor merely about "babysitting" kids.

As teacher educators, we have the complicated task of considering the ways in which our student teachers are learning (and unlearning) themselves while also helping them think about how their future students will learn (and unlearn) from their future teaching decisions and practices. Within this dynamic, multiple generations are implicated—each bringing different, albeit often related, understandings, cultural references, and discursive frameworks. This is quite visible when it comes to issues related to gender and sexuality as younger generations enter schools under changed conditions that provide particular novel, often legal, protections and recognitions. Although these protections and recognitions are limited and contested (including by religious arguments), it remains the case that young people bring their embodied selves into classrooms and that those selves are in formation and at times under assault when it comes not only to their sense of gender or sexuality but also to their sense of religion. There is very real tension present in the ways in which students' senses of sexual and gender becoming, as they run along different lines from binary, heteronormative expectations come into contact with religiously informed conservatism.

We began this chapter thinking about the oft-heard complaint of student teachers that they have to consider everything. On one hand, our argument here added yet another thing—the law and policy—for student teachers to consider. While school law and policy are more often the focus of policy and/or school administration programs, teacher education would do well to recognize the important role that the law plays in forming and informing the work of public education, the rights and protections of those involved, and the different ways those rights and protections play out. As we have shown, the law privileges the rights of students. Students are protected, at least nominally, from the state imposing any particular religious belief system on them, just as they are protected by the state from anti-LGBTQ violence and harassment. Things are less clear when it comes to the rights of teachers—be it for their religious identity or sexual orientation and gender identity—and it's even murkier for student teachers, who exist in the liminal space between two legally identified subject positions. The right to be out as teachers is affirmed but within particular parameters that are themselves under construction.

For student teachers, an educational task is to consider how their own subject position is in flux as they move more fully to the side of "teacher." Such consideration requires them to think through how they, as teachers, become subject to the law in a different way while simultaneously having to consider how their own students have different albeit related rights that are, themselves, evolving and changing. In doing this, we would do well to follow Phyllis's advice (Fendler, 2011) that we question our assumptions about what is good and seeking to do less harm next time. Within such work, we suggest a turn to forgiveness amid emerging discussions and debates about safe spaces, trigger warnings, and the challenges that happen at the interstices of fractured and fragmented discourses.

References

Abington School District v. Schempp, 374 U.S. 203 (1963).

Biegel, S. (2010). *The right to be out: Sexual orientation and gender identity in America's public schools.* University of Minnesota Press.

Biesta, G. J. (2014). *The beautiful risk of education.* Paradigm.

Black, D. (2020). *Schoolhouse burning: Public education and the assault on American democracy.* Hachette Book Group.

Bostock v. Clayton County, 140 S. Ct. 1731, 207 L. Ed. 2d 218 (2020).

Britzman, D. (2007). Teacher education as uneven development: Towards a psychology of uncertainty. *International Journal of Leadership in Education, 10*(1), 1–12.

Burbules, N. C., & Densmore, K. (1991). The limits of making teaching a profession. *Educational Policy, 5*(1), 44–63.

Colin v. Orange Unified School District, 83 F. Supp. 2d 1135 (C.D. Cal. 2000).

Cuban, L. (2013). *Inside the black box of classroom practice: Change without reform in American education.* Harvard Education Press.

Driver, J. (2018). *The schoolhouse gate: Public education, the Supreme Court, and the battle for the American mind.* Pantheon.

Duncan, A. (2011, June 14). *Dear colleagues.* US Department of Education. https://www2.ed.gov/policy/elsec/guid/secletter/110607.html

East High Gay Straight Alliance v. Board of Education of Salt Lake City School District, 30 F. Supp. 2d 1356 (D. Utah 1998).

Engel v. Vitale, 370 U.S. 421, 82 S. Ct. 1261 (1962).

Fendler, L. (2011). Edwin and Phyllis. *Studies in Philosophy and Education, 30*(5), 463–469.

Feiman-Nemser, S. (2012). *Teachers as learners.* Harvard Education Press.

Greteman, A. J. (2019). Non-advice for art educators engaging LGBTQ issues. *Art Education, 72*(2), 42–47.

Grimm v. Gloucester County School Board, 869 F.3d 286 (4th Cir. 2017).

Justice, B., & Macleod, C. (2016). *Have a little faith: Religion, democracy, and the American public school.* University of Chicago Press.

Koppelman, A. (2020). *Gay rights vs. religious liberty? The unnecessary conflict.* Oxford University Press.

Kosciw, J. G., Greytak, E. A., Zongrone, A. D., Clark, C. M., & Truong, N. L. (2018). *The 2017 National School Climate Survey: The experiences of lesbian, gay, bisexual, transgender, and queer youth in our nation's schools.* GLSEN.

Kunzman, R. (2006). Imaginative engagement with religious diversity in public school classrooms. *Religious Education, 101*(4), 516–530.

Labaree, D. (1997). *How to succeed at school without really learning: The credentials race in American education.* Yale University Press.

Labaree, D. (2010). *Someone has to fail: The zero-sum game of public schooling.* Harvard University Press.

Lawrence v. Texas, 539 U.S. 558, 123 S. Ct. 2472 (2003).

Lemon v. Kurtzman, 411 U.S. 192, 93 S. Ct. 1463 (1973).

Liptak, A. (2021, April 5). An extraordinary winning streak for religion at the supreme
    court. *New York Times.* https://www.nytimes.com/2021/04/05/us/politics/
    supreme-court-religion.html?referringSource=articleShare

Lortie, D. C. (1975). *Schoolteacher.* University of Chicago Press.

Marquez, R., & Brockenbrough, E. (2013). Queer youth v. the state of California:
    Interrogating legal discourses on the rights of queer students of color. *Curric-
    ulum Inquiry, 43*(4), 461-482.

Maxwell, S. (2021, February 5). To cover up anti-gay policies, Florida's voucher
    school industry has launched a new P.R. campaign. *Orlando Sentinel.* https://
    www.orlandosentinel.com/opinion/scott-maxwell-commentary/os-prem-
    op-gay-discrimination-florida-voucher-schools-scott-maxwell-20210205-
    2iiheettknapzp77xpmxl6wo5y-story.html

Mergens v. Board of Education, Westside Community. Schools, 867 F.2d 1076 (8th
    Cir. 1989).

Nabozny v. Podlesny, 92 7th Cir. 446 (1996).

National School Board Association. (2020). *Protections for LGBTQ employees and students
    after Boystock v. Clayton County: A new era in employment law and student rights.*

Plyler v. Doe, 457 U.S. 202, 102 S. Ct. 2382 (1982).

Riley, J. (2020, July 8). Supreme court says religious schools can fire LGBTQ employees
    despite nondiscrimination laws. *Metro Weekly.* https://www.metroweekly.com/
    2020/07/supreme-court-says-religious-schools-exempt-nondiscrimination-
    laws/

Rosky, C. J. (2013). Fear of the queer child. *Buffalo Law Review, 61*(3), 607–697.

Sanchez, M. (2019). *Queer faith: Reading promiscuity and race in the secular love tradition.*
    NYU Press.

Scopes v. State, 154 Tenn. 105, 126, 289 S.W. 363, 369 (1927).

Segall, A. (2002). *Disturbing practice: Reading teacher education as text.* Peter Lang
    Publishing.

Stone v. Graham, 449 U.S. 39, 101 S. Ct. 192 (1980).

Tyack, D., & Cuban, L. (1995). *Tinkering toward utopia: A century of public school reform.*
    Harvard University Press.

Trinity Lutheran v. Comer, 582 U.S. 137, 577 S. CT. 4061 (2017)

Wisconsin v. Yoder, 406 U.S. 205, 92 S. Ct. 1526 (1972).

Zelman v. Simmons-Harris, 536 U.S. 639, 122 S. Ct. 2460 (2002).

CHAPTER 5

Forgiveness Amid Difference

A Preliminary Conversation

Adam: Some things that seem to be defining features of education moving into the 2020s are "cancel culture," "safe spaces," and "trigger warnings." Each of these concepts has led to a proliferation of thought pieces, research, and educator angst. From fears that one might say or write something "wrong" to the existential dread that something from a profligate past might be unearthed to concerns that one will fail at providing trigger warnings and thus a "safe space," educators have been put on the spot in different ways by an activated student body. I think that some of these fears are generally overblown, although that's not to say that the *experience* of the fear isn't real. This is an important distinction, one between rhetoric and reality, we try, I hope, to hold onto throughout the book to both recognize the work of rhetoric alongside how such rhetorics play out in reality in classrooms between students and teachers. Still, given the precarious realities of many faculty, the specter of controversy emerges with more visible material consequences. For me, as I have already written, what seems needed amidst these fears and concerns is a return to and recognition of "education" (Greteman, 2020). I think that moments of cancellation, "safe spaces," and requests for trigger warnings can be read as "educational asks." They are, after all, situated in educational institutions and are emerging from students coming into presence, always. Yet, rather than seeing such requests or demands educationally, we tend to refract them through political discourses (student activism) or therapeutic discourses (concerns about student mental health), which, while important, I sense miss the educational potential of the asking.

What I am curious about alongside the potential of an "educational ask" is what happens after a failed trigger warning or what emerges subsequent to an individual being called out (or calling someone out). Those things are, after all, momentary. Where do we go after such moments, particularly given the reality that often "class" continues? So, to explore what happens after, we want to turn to apology and forgiveness. I think these twinned concepts are overplayed in the popular press, with apologies being released and forgiveness given immediately after a scandal or controversy breaks with little time to actually digest the controversy itself. One might look to the immediate aftermath of the insurrection at the Capitol building in the United States in January 2021, as Republican congresspeople and right-wing pundits, utilizing a well-worn trope, called for unity prior to and instead of accountability. Accountability is a precondition, we should be clear, for the kind of forgiveness we write about here. At that level—what I think of as the "cultural" level—apologies and forgiveness do particular work, often, it would seem, for "public relations" and "image control." Teacher educators (and educators writ large), however, are not, generally speaking, movers and shakers on the cultural level. Rather, we draw on the cultural level—films, artwork, pop culture, and so on—within and through the interpersonal level where we teach and create opportunities for students to think, make, and come into presence amid their cultural milieu. Teacher educators rarely reach a heightened level of cultural notoriety, which does not discount the work we do but, rather, suggests that we have a different task in front of us, namely, to educate students who are becoming teachers in their own regard to contribute to the work of public education themselves.

So, although apology and forgiveness become fodder on cultural landscapes, we want to think about the work of those actions—of apologizing, of forgiving—within teacher education. As teacher educators, how do we develop ways to help ourselves in relation to our students think about "apologies" and "forgiveness" such that they become both viable and visible practices within educational relations?

Kevin: One of the experiences along the way in growing up a certain kind of Catholic is the sacrament of Reconciliation. This typically occurs in or around second grade and requires some form of official education sanctioned by the church, which generally happens either in Catholic school or in the Confraternity of Christian Doctrine (CCD), which is a fancy way of saying, roughly, Sunday school for public school kids. Part of that preparation, from what I recall of my own CCD experience, was the anxiety of admitting to a priest your sins. Although the sacrament is, at base, about forgiveness, indeed reparation, and a washing away of the stain of sin on the soul, it's also, as

Foucault (2014) makes clear, "submission to another" (p. 165) and "verbalizing the self" (p. 167) as a certain kind of being: a sinner.

The theology, however, at age 8 or so, isn't quite so considered and what ends up happening is the dilemma of (a) admitting real "sins" such as they are in the second-grade mind, (b) making some up, or (c) finding none in the deep reflection on one's actions, going out and committing the kinds of sins that might need forgiving. When we have spoken about this chapter and our conversations have wandered, as they always do, we have continually returned to a sense of the possibility for grace. I had a professor as an undergraduate who, in a course called The Sacramental Principle, argued that the sacraments are instances when Catholics attend to God's grace extended beyond the Trinity. The trick, he said, is that there's nothing inherently sacramental about, for instance, the action of confessing to a priest that couldn't also be affected by attending to the grace of God in a moment in the parking lot of the church when a stranger causes you to find joy for a fleeting instant. It's just that we set aside particular moments, ritualized into importance, to purposefully focus our attention as a way to find grace through various sacraments. The ritual calls forth the grace that is, actually, always already there if only we were paying enough attention.

I suppose the idea means, in relation to this work here, that teaching, the coming into consciousness of the fact that students are putting forth educational asks that make us potentially uncomfortable, requires not an apology so much as an acknowledgment of the grace that already existed in the relationship that allowed for the calling out or, alternatively, the calling in. This seems better than inventing sins for the sake of seeking absolution whereby both parties might really be seeking the submission of the other. Still, apologies might also be required, but they can never merely be proforma lest it be really about producing a sinner for the sake of absolution rather than some other substantial relational change.

Adam: In play, I sense, is then a third act—that of acknowledging grace—and how it plays into those moments in education where relations face difficulty. Relations, particularly educational relations, I think always face difficulty at some juncture given the risks inherent in education. Or, to play off a safe-sex campaign, education without risk doesn't exist. So how do we think through the risks of teaching alongside the risks of learning and moments when those risks overwhelm us and potentially cause harm. I want to suggest, as we move into this exploration, that the work of forgiveness is central. But so will be, as the next chapter explores, reconciliation. Reconciliation, both as it plays out theologically and as an action of restoring relations, manifests not only in the "everydayness" of school but also through the evolving legal battles for "America's soul."

Framing Forgiveness

In the aftermath of the White supremacist terrorist attack during a Bible study at Emanuel African Methodist Episcopal Church in Charleston, South Carolina, in 2015, mere days after the murder of nine congregants, family members of those slain testified in court. A number of them offered the perpetrator forgiveness, as reported by Yahoo News (2015):

> "You took something really precious from me. I will never talk to her again," the daughter of 70-year-old Ethel Lance, one of nine people killed in the massacre, said. "But I forgive you and have mercy on your soul. You hurt me. You hurt a lot of people. But God forgives you. I forgive you." (para. 2)

Yet forgiveness was not easy for all survivors:

> "For me, I am a work in progress," admitted a relative of 49-year-old Depayne Middleton Doctor. "I am very angry, [but] we are the family that love built. We have no room for hate, so I have to forgive." (Yahoo News, 2015, para. 14)

Forgiveness became a central narrative in the aftermath as headlines across the United States highlighted how forgiveness offered a potential way through or past hatred. We should be clear, before moving on, that we don't question the sincerity or the healing possibility of the forgiveness offered in this particular case. Mourning is complex, and forgiveness in the case of the individuals here offered some redemptive possibilities amid pain.

However, the quick move to forgiveness did not sit well with everyone. Roxane Gay, in a *New York Times* op-ed titled "Why I Can't Forgive Dylann Roof," opposed the move and the perceived necessity of forgiving Roof, writing:

My unwillingness to forgive this man does not give him any kind of power. I am not filled with hate for this man because he is beneath my contempt. I do not believe in the death penalty so I don't wish to see him dead. My lack of forgiveness serves as a reminder that there are some acts that are so terrible that we should recognize them as such. We should recognize them as beyond forgiving. (para. 2)

Gay, like us, was raised Catholic, whereby forgiveness is an act the young are taught about through the sacrament of Reconciliation. One must confess one's sins and do penance. Through such work, one can gain forgiveness. One is not simply forgiven but has to work for it. This includes quite often reciting an act of contrition, any number of times dictated by the priest, often the Lord's Prayer. This is a prayer, as well, that was prayed for some time in America's public schools before litigation barred its utterance to maintain (or, more accurately, create) a veneer of separation between church and state. This history considered in the previous chapter aside, a key lesson from the Lord's Prayer includes the work of forgiveness: "and forgive us our trespasses as we forgive those who trespass against us." However, as Gay argues regarding this prayer,

> it's a nice idea that we could forgive those who might commit the same sins we are apt to commit, but surely there must be a line. Surely there are some trespasses most of us would not commit. What then? (para. 4)

What then, indeed? What happens when forgiveness is not an option because the mode of trespass has crossed a line beyond which we fail to see our own possible transgressions moving? Lines drawn, of course, are often redrawn as things change, as we change, but the questions in play persist. How do we respond to those who trespass against us? And similarly, how do we respond to those on whom we trespass?[1] On a personal level, this may be easy as we can draw our own individual lines. Yet the personal is quickly implicated with others and how any given line comes to encircle or mark the insuperability of those others. The personal may be political, where our personal choices make manifest our politics, but the ethical may be impersonal as we have to, in a sense, be able to see others at a remove from our own person. This, we suggest, is clear within schools where people meet and in meeting lines are drawn and crossed creating not only conflict but also abuse. These lines illuminate the ways the individual meets the collective and the private meets the public and the ways discourses, like forgiveness, deserve, as Gay opines, closer and more deliberative reflection.

In this chapter, we turn to lines drawn and lines crossed that affect the educational experiences of those impacted. And we do so, as a reminder, within the realm of teacher education, in which students and educators not only are implicated in contemplating their immediate "scene" of education but also are tasked with contemplating how such scenes will play out in student teachers' futures with their own students. Such contemplation is not singular but involves contemplating decisions, judgments, and punishments that always already raise important ethical and educational questions. What we want to suggest in following this line of inquiry is the use of a robust understanding of forgiveness, starting first with the work of hospitality. Forgiveness may inevitably not be possible, yet scenes of education continue, meaning we may need to grapple with how to engage (or not) hospitably with different ideas and modes of relating. Or, put differently, we may do well by exploring the work of opening ourselves to a hospitality to differences without the added pressures or expectations of forgiveness. Bluntly, we are not asking that those harmed by the most damaging discourses of religious extremism forgive the trespasses of its adherents or its theologies. We are asking that we think of ways in which we'll be required to be open, ourselves, to the presence of these ideas and people influenced by them in the ranks of our students. The question becomes, then, What next? What best ought we do?

Working the Hyphen

As we begin to think about the work of forgiveness and hospitality it is necessary to reiterate the interesting realities of teacher education. Teacher educators and their students enter into their relations amid a contested, complex, and contradictory terrain. Teacher education students, who are often called student teachers, exist on that hyphen that simultaneously separates and connects their two positions. They are students, on one hand, and still exist within an institutional relation as learners, subject to the pedagogies of their professors. On the other hand, they exist as teachers gaining experience teaching others in their placement sites, subjecting students to their emerging novice pedagogies. This hyphenated space pulls student teachers between their own concerns/needs as learners and a new concern for the learning of others. Or, put differently, as students our responsibility (roughly, although not only and not always) is for our own learning, but as teachers, our responsibility expands to include a responsibility for others, notably our students.

In our estimation, working this hyphen is a founding reality in teacher education. It is a reality that informs the challenges that exist within teacher education. On one hand, we can think of teacher education as a "hated field," as elucidated by Deborah Britzman (2007), for the ways teacher education often does not prepare student teachers for uncertainty. On the other hand, we can also think of teacher education as a site where possibilities persist for imagining and manifesting educational transformation within contexts. Amid the hyphenated work of being a student teacher, teacher educators are similarly placed in complicated positions given how they carry their own psychic baggage forward from their educations and are situated within an institution themselves. Teacher educators are, as well, in the process of learning to teach, an ongoing process, while also helping others learn to teach, as an ongoing process as well. Amid these realities and positions, both teacher educators and student teachers are finding ways to not only help others "learn" but are also cultivating forms of relations and grappling with uncertainties and uneven development. There are, we recognize here, a whole lot of "ifs" in this work. "If teacher education is to matter," Britzman concludes, "we are obligated to create conditions for learning to live in this time that is out of joint, in discontinuous time and the disjuncture of self/other relations" (2007, p. 11). Creating such conditions does not come with a prescribed set of rules and ideas but is rooted in having to take responsibility for the uncertainties and dependencies that are the very stuff of being human. Furthermore, as Britzman muses, drawing on Arendt, James, and Bion,

> if we are responsible for a world we have not made, if we have the
> strange work of trying to understand the minds of others and still
> keep our own mind, if we have the work of welcoming what cannot

be understood and the responsibility for a hospitality without re-
serve, if we confront a world that is wearing out, if we must work
from all this ignorance, we may then begin our teacher education.
(pp. 11–12)

We may then begin our teacher education amidst a series of recognitions
that limn the scene. We may then begin encountering and leaning into the
ever-present "ifs" that surround us. A central aspect of such work is the initial
moment, perhaps gesture, of welcoming those whom we meet in our classrooms.
This asks us to think through hospitality.

On Hospitality

Jen Gilbert (2006), in concluding an engagement with Derrida's work on
hospitality, pondered: "If education is a relation of hospitality, then we will
affect and be affected by our encounters with others" (p. 33). Gilbert's conditional statement doesn't declare that education is a relation of hospitality but
opens up an opportunity to think through such a supposition. Supposing that
we see education as a relation of hospitality, then what? Before getting to her
supposition, Gilbert explored Derrida's understanding of hospitality to wrestle,
in particular, "gayness" from "scandal" and "controversy." Gayness, as Gilbert
maintains, operated within education as something controversial. Where gayness reared its head, controversy was sure to follow. Recognizing the limitations
of "controversy," she turned to hospitality and what it brings to the scene of
education. In doing so, she sought to shift the conversation away from a "time
of difficulty"—wherein when gayness entered education, difficulty ensued—to
a "time of hospitality"—wherein gayness became conceptualized as "central to
the work of learning" (p. 26). The centrality of gayness to the work of learning
entered Gilbert's argument because of the ways in which gayness impacts education when and how it arrives on the scene. Its arrival—if reframed around
hospitality instead of difficulty—creates an opportunity to not simply think
about a discrete identity or sexual practices. Rather, "gayness is a quality of
experience: it imbues all of one's relationships with the world" (p. 26). Gayness
arrives in scenes of education, but such an arrival needs a different conceptual

framework to understand it not only as difficult but as central to education's project as well. We think, in ways that are important but not syllogistic, that religion in teacher education might be treated similarly. Religious conceptions of self matter deeply to our student teachers (and to their students and to their professors), and this is treated as both controversial and limiting in teacher education classrooms—if it's addressed at all. What, we wonder, are we to do with a call for hospitality for gayness if we are to shift that call to thinking with and about religiousness in our spaces? Again, these are not equal considerations complicated by histories and material consequences of those histories, but failing to think about how we will welcome what shows up in religious form, and what we will do with it and the people who bear it leaves us wholly unprepared for the reality of student identity and eventual student-teacher practice.

Gilbert's assessment and intervention were of their own time, namely, the mid-2000s, amid a variety of battles for "gay rights." Such battles persist but have also evolved. To stay within the U.S. context, since the mid-2000s we have seen the federal recognition of marriage for same-sex couples, in 2015's *Obergefell*, the continued expansion of Gay-Straight Alliances or Gender and Sexuality Alliances (GSAs), and the inclusion of gender identity and sexual orientation as protected within employment (via Title VII) through the 2020 *Bostock* decision. Along with these, we have seen an expansion in media representations of LGBTQ+ people and an increase in the number of states—five at the time of this writing—that mandate LGBTQ+ content in public education curricula.[2] The conceptual resources now available have changed. The quality of experience, as such, has evolved in ways that point toward a certain changed environment, a more "hospitable" environment, for not only those who identify as "LBGTQ" but, more generally, given the ways in which sexuality and gender are universalized encounters as well. This changed environment, to be clear, while more hospitable in some regards remains hostile in other regards (Kosciw et al., 2018).

Such an evolved environment, more hospitable while still hostile, however, does not disrupt the "time of hospitality" and its needs from teachers. Rather, the time of hospitality as supposed by Gilbert (2006) persists amid needs for different conceptual resources. However, before we get to such needs at the dawn of the 2020s, let us review Gilbert's argument.

"When standing at the door of education," Gilbert (2006) asks, "who will be invited in and under what conditions?" (p. 26). The question of who and under what conditions frames the challenges presented by hospitality. Hospitality, as understood by Derrida, operates on contested terrain between laws and the Law. Laws, or more so laws, with a lowercase *l*, are those human inventions rooted in politics and the judicial realm while the Law, with a capital *L*, exists as an ideal. Neither laws nor the Law can be reduced to one another, but neither can exist alone. As such, for Gilbert, "the insistence for pedagogy is that ethics resides in that perverted space between laws and the Law" (p. 28). Education, as a relation of hospitality, put differently, is where teachers and students in their everydayness "wrestle with the difficult question of how to turn our abstract commitment to hospitality into pedagogical practices that express, in albeit imperfect ways, that commitment" (p. 29). A commitment, again, to say "yes to whoever or whatever turns up."

The time of hospitality is a time of navigating the ever-present space between a stated ideal and empirical realities. Such realities rooted in politics, histories, policies, and laws make possible moments of hospitality, hence our earlier comment about the evolved quality of experiences and conceptual resources around "gayness." However, in making possible such changes and evolutions, exclusions remain, holding open the space between the "empirical" and the "ideal." For Gilbert (2006), education is a key space in which such navigation ensues as teachers and students seek to, amid their relations, carve out space for not only their "being" but also their "becoming." The ethical work of hospitality meets immediately the ontological work of being and becoming. The gap between our empirical realities and our ideals is where conflict is present both ethically (how we relate to others) and ontologically (how we become subjects). Gilbert seeks, through her turn to hospitality, "to see hospitality as necessarily emerging from the conflict between what we imagine and what we can do, and to insist that our commitment to justice and human rights does not, and indeed cannot, lie flush with social practices" (p. 33). Hospitality, as a universal Law, frames the challenge of educational relations both by requiring that we see education as "relational" and by setting us up to see the work at hand as never complete, as always already operating in conflict between our ideals and our realities.

The conflict between our ideals and our realities impacts not only how we relate to others but also what we are able to relate to others as. For Gilbert

(2006), gayness set up a way to recognize the need for and challenges that arise in education given the realities that faced "gayness" as it manifested in schools. Subjects who identify as or are perceived to be "gay" enter scenes of education as "strangers" to the given normative landscape. In a "time of difficulty" framed by controversy, such subjects encounter forms of exclusion and violence that seek to "straighten" them out to fit within that given "reality." However, in her call for hospitality, Gilbert offers a different framework that does not eliminate conflict and risk but, rather, recognizes the conflict and risk as inherent to the work of education. Alongside hospitality, as a starting point for the scene of education in which we "say yes to who or what turns up," we want to turn as well to contemplate what happens after we say "yes." Our yes, after all, will usher in different students and ideas that change over time and require that we, as educators, work through our own uncertainties and biases.

Like Gilbert, a grounding assumption for our work is that education is a relation of hospitality. This ethical starting point and its ambivalence, we think, does justice to the complex and contradictory space of schools and the relations that result from engagement in that space and time. The work of education is relational work as it is within education that we come to know not only "things," others, and ourselves but also how we relate to and feel about those things, others, and selves. We learn within education how to relate to others and ourselves. And these relations and thoughts are intimately tied to our feelings. Hospitality, as a framework, sets up our arrival into education to be radically open while recognizing the immediate empirical limitations on our arrival. These include limitations established by laws, politics, morals, and more. Within these scenes, risks are taken and conflicts emerge as decisions are made. This leaves us to ponder what happens after we say yes. If we say yes to who or what turns up, how does such a "yes" play out as teachers and students wrestle with the conflict that emerges *between* our "ideals," or what we imagine, and our "reality," or what we can do? In education, as is perhaps obvious, we have to do something. And in doing something, we have to consider the things we choose to do. In doing something, we open ourselves and our students up to unforeseen and unexpected experiences. What happens when those experiences lead to not just conflict but also harm whether such harm is real or imagined? How do we come back from such conflict or the harm it has caused within the educational relation?

To explore this, we turn to forgiveness as a possible response to conflict and harm. In the next chapter, we take up the possibility of reconciliation. We first explore forgiveness, following Gilbert's lead, by turning to Derrida. The work of Michalenos Zembylas (2007) helps bridge this chapter's focus on forgiveness and our next chapter's engagement with reconciliation—particularly his work articulating a pedagogy of forgiveness and reconciliation. It is important to remember that our interest is not in dictating who or what receives forgiveness but, rather, to think with the language of forgiveness and its potential in navigating the happenings in classrooms as such happenings unfold in complex ways.

On Forgiveness

Derrida and his deconstructive work on forgiveness at first glance to newcomers might seem overly obtuse, particularly within teacher education where students (and often professors) want to know the use value of an idea to help "teach on Monday." However, "deconstruction is," taking a lesson from Critchley and Kearney (2001), "not some obscure textual operation . . . but is a concrete intervention in contexts that is governed by an undeconstructable concern for justice" (p. viii). Deconstruction is recognized here as a form of intervention that seeks to interrupt our everyday lifeworlds. It is, of course, not the only form of intervention needed but, rather, a form of intervention that also draws our attention to the working of concepts and our ability to engage such concepts within our practices. As Gilbert's engagement with Derrida earlier showed, a concept such as hospitality is far from straightforward but, rather, exists within contradictions, histories, and heritages. Concepts, put differently, on close engagement, present their paradoxes. And while we might wish to overcome such paradoxes, Derrida allows us to reconcile ourselves to the reality that it is the paradoxical nature of concepts that maintains the need for continued vigilance in our work. The paradoxes of concepts like hospitality or forgiveness maintain our ethical and political work as educators meeting others in the world.

Forgiveness is, as Derrida noted, an "enigmatic concept." Definitions of forgiveness vary, contributing to this enigmatic status. Most definitions of forgiveness, however, as Zembylas (2007) maintains, "agree that forgiveness is a moral virtue or power that has mainly to do with a change of heart and consequently a change of a particular relationship" (p. 83). Despite such general agreement, it remains the case that forgiveness is no simple matter. Derrida's own engagement with forgiveness was rooted within its historical moment as forgiveness was being globalized with nation-states, corporations, and sovereigns asking forgiveness. This was seen notably through South Africa's Truth and Reconciliation Commission. As forgiveness was being asked for at such a scale, forgiveness needed to be questioned and unpacked so as not to become trivialized. Such questioning did not simplify forgiveness but illustrated its complexities and contradictions: What is forgiveness? Who can give it? Who can ask for it? Is forgiveness meant for an "act" or for a "person"? and so on. No particular response to these questions can settle the questions once and for all; rather, they allow us to see the contextual and contingent realities that are always already present when considering the concept, including the important ways forgiveness implicates memory.

For Derrida (2001a), there is an aporia, a paradox, at the heart of forgiveness. "Forgiveness," as he articulated, "only becomes possible from the moment it appears impossible" (p. 37). Or, as he also wrote, "there is only forgiveness if there is any, where there is the unforgivable. That is to say that forgiveness must announce itself as impossibility itself. It can only be possible in doing the impossible" (p. 33). This paradoxical formulation sets up two poles to be considered. These two poles—between "conditional" and "unconditional" or "ideal" and "empirical"—are not reconcilable but "must remain irreducible" (p. 45?). They are "shifty enough not to . . . be determined as simple opposition" (Derrida, 2001b, p. 45). Forgiveness, in the pure sense, "is mad," meaning "that an act of forgiveness worthy of its name, if there ever was such a thing, must forgive the unforgivable, and without condition" (Derrida, 2001a, p. 39). This madness, as Zembylas (2007) points out, illustrates how "unconditional forgiveness is what grants meaning to the entire discourse of forgiveness" (p. 85). Forgiveness means something because in its pure sense, it does something unimaginable that maintains our ability to think through forgiveness's complexities and make decisions about what and if to forgive. This, of course, is what Gay struggled with and, at least temporarily, refused in the case of Dylann Roof.

A complexity of particular interest within discourses of forgiveness is the role and work of memory. As Derrida (2001a) points out, forgiveness "signifies, no doubt, a universal urgency of memory" (p. 28). Forgiveness implicates the past, implicates our memories of being wronged (or wronging an other). To ask for forgiveness implies a recognition of this past, a memory of causing harm or trauma. With forgiveness comes, as is often imagined, "forgetting" in the well-worn phrase "forgive and forget." Yet, in "To Forgive: The Unforgivable and the Imprescriptible," Derrida (2001b) makes clear that "forgiving is not forgetting" (p. 23) since the notion creates an exchange whereby upon granting forgiveness one forgets. This not only upends Derrida's notion of pure forgiveness but also touches on his thoughts on forgetting. As Zembylas (2007), drawing on Derrida, points out, "both forgiveness and forgetting are acts of responsibility and thus the (endless) ethical responsibility is to forgive and forget, remembering the past, being critical of it, and working through it" (p. 87). Forgiving and forgetting here are not dependent on one another. Rather, they are different acts that each engages the past and memory. Forgetting is not an act of refusing to remember but an act of working through memory to get somewhere else. We might forgive and forget in sequence, but each requires its own unique work. Both operate independently of the other to do work in the world with others.

Pure forgiveness, as an ideal and unconditional concept, exists in tension with forgiveness as it exists in our everyday realities. Conditional forgiveness is, put simply, the form of forgiveness we are generally most familiar with as it is called on within an exchange. Conditional forgiveness comes with conditions and to happen such conditions must be met. This is similar to the paradox of hospitality engaged by Gilbert earlier. This conflict between an unconditional view of forgiveness that "must forgive the unforgivable and without condition" (Derrida, 2001a, p. 39) butts up against the conditions of our lives. What are we to make, then, of this paradox between unconditional and conditional forgiveness as we make decisions about forgiveness in education specifically? Richard Bernstein (2006) argues that a key task is "to insist that deciding what is really unforgivable is always a *contestable* issue that is fraught with difficulties" (p. 400). There is not, nor will there be, a stable understanding. Rather, it is working through the issues in play and the contestations that will inevitably emerge. Or, as teachers will recognize from their workaday worlds, it depends.

For Derrida (2001a), this is the very work of the aporia of forgiveness. We are to make decisions by experiencing the paradox of forgiveness and the issues such a paradox raises. As he argues, the aporia is the experience of responsibility. It is only by going through a set of contradictory injunctions, impossible choices, that we make a choice. If I know what I have to do, if I know in advance what has to be done, then there is no responsibility. For the responsible decision envisaged or taken, we have to go through pain and aporia, a situation in which I do not know what to do. I have to do this and this, and they do not go together. I have to face two incompatible injunctions, and that is what I have to do every day in every situation, ethical, political, or not. (p. 62)

Every day and in every situation, teachers and students encounter one another. Often, such encounters pass by unnoticed. Yet, such encounters also lead to moments where differences come to the fore and require more complicated conversations and decisions to be made. Not all of our decisions will end up being the so-called right decisions, provoking us to return to the ethical work of questioning what we think is good and altering possible future decisions.

Affective Pedagogies of Forgiveness

There are innumerable moments in a classroom that can or cannot lead in any possible directions as decisions are made (and therefore other decisions are not made). Conflict, of course, can emerge in and around such decisions as they reveal all kinds of issues, some that might seem rather minor and others that seem more major, although, in the moment, such distinctions between minor and major issues generally fall by the wayside to make room for engaging in the work at hand. In such moments in a classroom, moments we imagine any teacher might immediately be able to recall, the affective atmosphere often becomes charged. Emotions run high, asking those involved to navigate the affective realities of education, including as we started to address earlier, the feelings that hover around forgiveness.

Michalinos Zembylas (2007), in *Five Pedagogies, a Thousand Possibilities*, turns to a relational understanding of emotions, contributing to a push for engaging the work of emotions in education. Such engagement is not simple given the ways in which emotions have often not only been individualized through psychological discourses but are also pushed to the edges of education's work in distinction from, for instance, the work of therapy. Amid such complexities, Zembylas threads together an argument that seeks to wrestle with the always already present emotional landscapes of education to illustrate the politics of emotions and their necessary use in education.

Zembylas's (2007) exploration is one rooted in hope, particularly critical hope, which "is grounded in careful critical analysis and an understanding of how emotional attachments, historical circumstances, and material conditions have led us to the present, and signifies a willingness to be open to the implications of this analysis" (pp. xvi–xvii). Within educational relations then, Zembylas argues, critical hope,

> inspires teachers and students to see patterns in their emotional, historical, and material lives, to realize how these patterns are made and what their consequences are for maintaining the status quo, and to motivate teachers and students to position themselves critically. (p. xii)

Critical hope brings together criticality and emotionality to wrestle with the ever-present tensions that exist within our everyday educational lives. And for those of us interested in and committed to ideas of justice, critical hope assists both teachers and students in grappling with "tensions between seeing possibilities and limits, the hopes and disappointments of the choices one makes" (Zembylas, 2007, p. xvi). Choices, after all, have to be made, and how those choices play out is the stuff of educational relations.

However, within our current educational conditions, these relations are strained as educational institutions grapple with legacies of exclusion and activated student and teacher bodies demanding change. Education is—in various institutional guises—increasingly policed, be that through changing ideas of school reform, the contested presence of actual police within schools, the presence of digital media documenting classrooms, and so forth. Techniques of surveillance and policing alter the educational landscape broadly and specifically contribute to complicated relations, including a certain paranoia between not only students and teachers but also teachers and administration.

Within teacher education, these diverse forms of policing impact how and what the field does or can do. Teacher education is, of course, a set of relations between not only teacher educators and student teachers but also mentor teachers, local school districts, policymakers, community constituents, and broader discourses about and around what education should entail. And on any given day, as already noted, in the United States, a vast swathe of the population is involved with public education. These relations—general as they may be in writing—exist within specific contexts and under specific conditions, which is to say that while we might wish we could develop "best practices" that do away with tensions and struggle, the sheer vastness of education as an administrative feat beautifully thwarts us. But it also calls for thinking through the work of forgiveness as an act, even an impossible act, that can do something within these conditions.

Given this, we recognize the reality that struggle and possibility are constitutive of our lives. This is not to romanticize struggle nor possibility. Rather, it is to ground ourselves in our ever-present and ever-changing work within teacher education. Such work is not solely about developing our "minds," but is instead intimately connected to our bodies and hearts. As such, "we are asked" by Zembylas (2007) "to consider how teachers and students can create classroom spaces that enable productive critical and pedagogical scenes of witnessing while foregrounding the ungovernability of affects" (p. xix). Spaces are created in and over time as students and teachers navigate the scene's unfolding, with all involved playing roles that impact the unfolding itself. Teacher educators make choices about how student teachers are brought into not only the "profession" but also the everyday work that goes into teaching. We, as teacher educators, make choices about how student teachers are oriented toward some objects and bodies and away from others. We do not prescribe any particular objects or bodies here; rather, we want to recognize and explore the need to address how those choices provoke not only critical thinking and action but also emotions.

Again, such emotions are not to be understood as individualized states but as emerging within relations. In our work, these are educational relations that, through teaching and learning, develop in heterogeneous ways. Furthermore, relations change with and over time as different choices are made and new dynamics encountered. For us, this is part of the joy of teaching in that it allows for a sustained encounter and engagement with students that is never static, always dynamic. Such encounters are, as any educator knows, never entirely one way or another, but defined by their complexities and tensions. They are, as well, intimately tied to the emotional landscape that exists within any given classroom. For Zembylas (2007),

> we—that is teachers, students, parents, and all those involved in the educational process—and the lifeworlds we invent are the ones who move and [are] moved by provocative or complicit images and imaginations of various pedagogies. (p. xv)

Movement—both physical and emotional—is central to scenes of education as the objects and bodies involved move about their work, are moved by curricular choices, and move one another through our individual contributions to the overall environment of a class.

What Zembylas illuminates in his work are the ways in which scenes of education—in their everydayness—are oriented toward and therefore away from different objects and bodies. The ways our choices orient or how the choices of others orient not only what we see and think about but also how or what we feel. The work of orienting is not only spatial—implicating the ways in which we can turn away from objects or bodies—but also emotional. We are moved by those things that we encounter; we may assign those things that we are moved by; we might learn that what moves us moves others differently. And, amid these movements, we are similarly moved away from other things that retreat from our view.

Such movement illuminates the dynamic nature of education. And it illuminates, as well, why Zembylas is so focused on bringing together the need to address the complexities and tensions within this dynamic. To engage in the work of education is to engage hearts, bodies, and minds. Yet such engagement is never not already implicated in broader historical, philosophical, and material conditions. And as Zembylas (2007) points out,

> Learning to think, feel, and relate differently is both an existential and an ethical task which requires that individuals stand outside a particular set of beliefs and assumptions that offer comfort and certainty to them and recognize how one has been taught to accept particular ideologies and feel about them. (p. xxviii)

This is easier written than done, in part, because writing allows ideas to sediment themselves while teaching and learning are never settled, always in flux in the flow of relationship. However, what Zembylas reminds us about are the risks that are entailed in learning, if we are to learn in ways that challenge rather than merely affirm our already present viewpoints and ideas.

Risk is ever present when religion, sexualities, and genders enter the frame. On one hand, each of these is always already present since we cannot leave our religious, sexual, or gender identities at the school entrance. On the other hand, each of these is implicated implicitly or explicitly within the choices that schools and their teachers make. These choices orient students toward ideas and objects and away from others. Of course, from either "left"- or "right"-wing ideologies, choices that schools and teachers make are broadly disparaged. Public schools either propagate lies (the left's accusations) or peddle in left-wing wokeness (the right's accusations). The truth is somewhere present in these discourses, although not wholly exclusive to either. And we are comfortable with such an idea, to embody Zembylas's sense that learning is an existential and ethical task that both forms and informs our "existence" and relations to others.

Power and Forgiveness

A challenge that teacher educators face within such a constellation of issues revolves around the ways students bring to classrooms their own changed and charged ideas emanating not only from their time in school but also their time immersed in other modes of education. These complexities raise questions about power that have been for the last half a century and more a component of educational scholarship. Yet, as Pinar (2013) reminds us, we cannot take such decades of scholarship on power for granted, in part, because doing so does a certain injustice to thinking about power as it changes in the midst of evolving contexts and conditions. There may be, on a certain rhetorical level, a belief in the power of forgiveness. Yet, as we have shown above, the power of forgiveness is far from determined. Patricia Hill Collins (2009), in *Another Kind of Public Education*, offers a four-part framework to think about power as it operates in different domains. Collins, who addresses legacies of racism and antiracist practices within education, illustrated a way to think through the complexities always present in schools, schools that are implicated in a range of power dynamics, including the ways if and how forgiveness is granted or offered.

Collins's (2009) Domains of Power are divided into four parts, each allowing us to think through a component implicated in oppression and its opposition. These four parts include the structural, the disciplinary, the cultural, and the interpersonal. The structural domain looks at the structures, read institutions, such as schools, courts, and hospitals, where people meet and the ways such institutions structure relations of power (student/teacher; judge/litigant; doctor/patient). The disciplinary domain looks at the policies and laws that frame the ways people can act, disciplining, so to speak, human interactions. The cultural domain gets at works of culture including film, television, social media, and more that create and tell stories about people. Finally, the interpersonal domain addresses the interactions between people, on the ground, where the other domains are always already in play. For Collins, this framework sought to push against the move to frame racism as only an issue in the interpersonal domain, which not only often led to defensiveness by those labeled "racists" (i.e., "But, I'm not a racist. I have lots of 'x kind' of friends") but failed to address the ways racism operated on different domains.

Over a decade after Collins laid out this framework, there has been success in expanding the conversation to address systemic racism as it emerges through institutions, policies, and cultural production. This shift asks that educators themselves think through not just their interpersonal dynamics with students-as-other but also the ways in which the conditions of education, already implicated in the four domains, require an expanded form of responsibility. Such work is never easy nor singular as students and teachers bring with them a range of identities that butt up against others and their own sense of self. We see this, perhaps most clearly, when we look at contemporary debates about trigger warnings and cancel culture that raise questions not only about the interpersonal but also the cultural, disciplinary, and structural domains that condition educational dynamics.

Triggering Differences

As students enter classrooms, they do so with access to concepts and ideas that may or may not be recognized or fully understood by educators. This requires continued attention to broad generational shifts and the very real work of both helping students comprehend the world they were born into while not submitting to that world. Here we think of concepts as similar to frames for apprehending the world; ideas flow through frames as we come to understand the world and work toward its transformation. For Foucault, we might think of these as ideologies and discourses: certain ideologies make particular discourses im/possible, just as a given concept ("I love students," for instance) will lead to particularized ideas about how to act in the world ("I must treat them thusly in the classroom"). Students' access to changed ideas and concepts are, as we could expect, limited and in development. They are students in school after all, receiving an education, meaning that the learning process is underway as they work to make sense of their curriculum.

However, one need only look at the cottage industry of books decrying the changing work of education to see how the demands made by students, in the general direction of a more inclusive and sensitive classroom, have caused a decades-long series of crises for the establishment. The charged realities of students coming into the world have plagued educational relations and purposes. From Arthur Bestor's (1953) so-called retreat from learning in 1950s' America to the "closing of the American mind" à la Allan Bloom (1987) and Greg Lukianoff and Jonathan Haidt's (2018) "coddling of the American mind" in the 2010s, differences within education have created conflict. If such arguments are to be believed, America's education systems have for decades been, in different ways, "failing" to live up to some imagined purpose, as they retreat, close, and coddle "America's minds" by narrowing or changing what happens in schools to the chagrin of mostly elite (White and male) gatekeepers. Such arguments, on face value, rest on some prelapsarian past in which education was great, whereby a return to such greatness is needed to "advance" or "open" or "uncoddle" America's minds and avoid setting up the next generation of such minds for failure. This was the basis of the back-to-basics movement in the 1970s and 1980s and its progenitors like the Committee of Ten at the turn of the 20th century. We're not breaking ground here suggesting that some certain conservative reactions to educational change and, perhaps, progress, is, well, reactionary. What we do suggest, however, is that we might understand the use value of such arguments a bit differently and respond accordingly.

Rhetorically, such arguments are provocative as they are returned to over and over again to confirm the continued downhill slide of education in the face of the dear old halcyon days of something better. Amid such provocations, however, these arguments provide a signpost for the changing work of education and the tensions present within any given educational moment and context. Our current moment—one of supposed "coddling"—is defined by arguments about trigger warnings and safe spaces. And these concepts and the hand-wringing that follows with them inform the experiences of both educators and students as they not only come into educational spaces but also come into their own selves. Educators express anxiety and fear about students' requests for trigger warnings or demands for safe spaces while students express anxiety and fear that they do not belong, don't feel safe, and cannot see themselves within the curriculum they must endure.

We, ourselves, are not actually interested in the arguments that posit an irrevocable lurch to the left in education or in opponents' counterarguments as we sense both stances are robustly, if unevenly, represented already. We hope to think with the idea that there are more than two sides to such a story. Those who rail loudest against coddling exaggerate their arguments and draw on limited extreme examples, often from elite campuses, while those who coddle through a firm belief in trigger warnings and safe spaces simplify the educational work in play and discount the complexity and agency of students. In previous work, Greteman has argued to the side of these to articulate the educational ask in play. "Trigger warnings," as he (2020) argues,

> are less a sign of the coddling of the American mind and more a sign of the continued challenges of doing the work of education as it comes to grapple with new bodies—literal bodies of students and their expanding bodies of knowledge. Trigger warnings, drawing on the expansion of who is in school, what and whose knowledge is taught, alongside the complex, often violent histories that are implicated in school, are central to uncoddling the American mind as it engages new and ever-emerging disciplines. This uncoddling is less

about the minds of students who are in the midst of learning how
to think and becoming subjects, but about adults who are unable
to meet such requests as educational; interpreting such requests instead as political, as a sign of fragility, or a refusal to engage. (p. 121)

While the polemical engagements with trigger warnings stoke further
debate, what they miss are the contexts and conditions in which such asks
are made. And they are made within scenes of education that involve an ever-expanding, diverse student body alongside a diversifying but still broadly
homogeneous teaching force.

To bring this chapter to a close, we want to propose that forgiveness might
offer a way through, not because forgiveness fixes anything but, rather, exposes
the paradox in play as students struggle to take up critical discourses that not
only contribute to their own sense of self but also assist in the work of reframing
the work of knowledge. Yet, since students are in the midst of this complex and
challenging work, there remains a need for working with students to engage
forgiveness themselves. This forgiveness will vary depending on the context,
but the role of forgiveness is to maintain space for students and teachers to not
be pitted against one another but to engage in the work of education responsibly. Responsibility will not fall on constituents evenly but will itself require
those involved to unpack the ways trigger warnings expose the fragmentation
of universal narratives and stories to instead begin to develop alternatives for
the creation of new kinds of narratives and stories. Such fragmentation will not
offer us a return to some prelapsarian past but, rather, will assist in collaging
together new possibilities that will themselves change and fragment in time.
This, we suggest, will ask that we reconcile ourselves to these fragmented conditions and refuse to idealize a past that rested on certainty. And to be clear, we
see neither forgiveness nor reconciliation as a process that forces us to let go of
a kind of righteous anger against injustice that might make us resist their more
sedate conceptual interpretations over time. For indeed, we believe along with
Goss (1993) that "queer anger is holy anger" (p. 177), which will require venting
along the way as well.

Endnotes

1 There is, readers of different denominations will note, an alternative version of the prayer that replaces *trespasses* with *debts*. The possibility for alternate readings intrigues us—rather than a harmful act, we might imagine something owed. We find the economic implications particularly interesting as well as the clear calls in the Bible to forgive fiscal indebtedness as a matter of course for Christians.
2 These include California, New Jersey, Illinois, Colorado, and Oregon.

References

Bernstein, R. (2006). Derrida: The aporia of forgiveness. *Constellations, 13*(3), 394–406.

Bestor, A. (1953). *Educational wastelands: The retreat from learning in our public schools.* University of Illinois Press.

Bloom, A. (1987). *Closing the American mind: How higher education has failed democracy and impoverished the souls of today's students.* Simon & Schuster.

Bostock v. Clayton County, 140 S. Ct. 1731, 207 L. Ed. 2d 218 (2020).

Britzman, D. (2007). Teacher education as uneven development: Towards a psychology of uncertainty. *International Journal of Leadership in Education, 10*(1), 1–12.

Collins, P. H. (2009). *Another kind of public education: Race, schools, the media, and democratic possibilities.* Beacon Press.

Critchley, S., & Kearney, R. (2001). Preface. In J. Derrida, *On cosmopolitanism and forgiveness* (pp. vii–xii). Routledge.

Derrida, J. (2001a). *On cosmopolitanism and forgiveness.* Routledge.

Derrida, J. (2001b). To forgive: The unforgivable and the imprescriptible. In J. D. Caputo, M. Dooley, & M. J. Scanlon (Eds.), *Questioning God* (pp. 21–51). Indiana University Press.

Foucault, M. (2014). *Wrong-doing, truth-telling: The function of avowal in justice* (S. W. Sawyer, Trans.; F. Brion & B. E. Harcourt, Eds.). University of Chicago Press.

Gay, R. (2015, June 23). Why I can't forgive Dylann Roof. *New York Times.* https://www.nytimes.com/2015/06/24/opinion/why-i-cant-forgive-dylann-roof.html

Gilbert, J. (2006). "Let us say yes to who or what turns up": Education as hospitality. *Journal of the Canadian Association for Curriculum Studies, 4*(1), 25–34.

Goss, R. E. (1993). *Jesus acted up. A gay and lesbian manifesto.* Harper.

Greteman, A. J. (2020). Uncoddling the American mind: The educational ask of trigger warnings. *Philosophy of Education, 2019*, 117–129.

Kosciw, J. G., Greytak, E. A., Zongrone, A. D., Clark, C. M., & Truong, N. L. (2018). *The 2017 National School Climate Survey: The experiences of lesbian, gay, bisexual, transgender, and queer youth in our nation's schools.* GLSEN.

Lukianoff, G., & Haidt, J. (2018). *The coddling of the American mind: How good intentions and bad ideas are setting up a generation for failure.* Penguin Press.

Obergefell v. Hodges, 135 S. Ct. 2584, 192 L. Ed. 2d 609 (2015)

Pinar, W. (2013). *Curriculum studies in the United States.* Palgrave Macmillan.

Yahoo News. (2015, June 19). *Families of Charleston shooting victims to Dylann Roof: We forgive you.* Yahoo News. https://news.yahoo.com/familes-of-charleston-church-shooting-victims-to-dylann-roof--we--forgive-you-185833509.html

Zembylas, M. (2007). *Five pedagogies, a thousand possibilities: Struggling for hope and transformation in education.* Brill.

CHAPTER 6

Reconciling Subjects

A Preliminary Conversation

Adam: Part of the work of writing is recognizing that writing is writing what you do not know until it is written. I think Lynn Fendler taught me this at some point during my doctoral education as I was finding my way into writing. I've carried this nugget of insight with me, not only reminding myself that writing is writing what I don't know until it is written but also paying the advice forward to my own students. As we have written this book together, this lesson returned to remind me that there are all sorts of emotions wrapped up in it along with an evolving sense of identity. Or, to put it differently, writing what you don't know until it is written asks one to stay with feelings of uncertainty, confusion, and the unknown with the hope that you will find yourself somewhere you didn't expect to find yourself. It is, in a simple sense I think, the process of reconciliation, of restoring a sense of friendliness to one's often contradictory and complex sense of self. As we navigated this work together—writing into what we don't know until it is written—I found myself needing to turn back to think about "teacher identity," which implicitly involves thinking about our own "teacher identity" as teacher educators. I don't, as this chapter explores, buy into a stable sense of identity, finding something more compelling within poststructural understandings of the subject that in many ways complicate identity talk. I am, as such, more compelled by the concept of becoming a subject due to the poetic ways in which the word subject operates within a Foucauldian framework and how reconciliation might offer a way into some form of restoration between competing ideologies and the tensions they create.

For this chapter, I am really interested in the work of "teacher identity" as it comes into conflict with competing discourses in education. By this, I am curious about how a shared dynamic between "queer" and "religious" teachers of being told to "keep such things private" butts up against the demands of professionalism and its public. Queer and religious identities are often thought of separately but are embodied together in our sense of self. And each of them overlaps, differs from, and informs the other. A central concern for this book is contemplating ways to navigate these overlaps and differences.

Kevin: My mom, now in her late 70s, has maintained in conversations with me throughout my teaching career—first as a high school English and religion teacher, a writing instructor at the university level, and then as a teacher educator across three institutions—that people are just *born* teachers. She references, by way of example, my sister Julie, who has long been a middle school English language arts teacher, as well as her daughter Erin, my niece, who teaches middle-grades science. Both of these women are good—and they are *really* good—teachers because of their inborn teacherliness.

Mom graduated from Mundelein College in Chicago, back before it was absorbed by Loyola University, and although she majored in history, in the early 1960s, when she attended, it was clearly assumed that this degree would lead a young woman into the classroom at least until she married. And that's what happened: She taught fifth grade for a year, and then, pregnant with my oldest sister, left the profession and spent the next 36 years working as a stay-at-home mother of five. She was, in every sense of the word, a teacher in her career as a mother but uncompensated in the ways that tend to matter for prestige that's anything but symbolic. And still, she maintains that, all those years ago in that Catholic school on the north side of Chicago, she realized that she wasn't cut out to teach. She wasn't born with it.

This notion of a congenital teacher identity isn't an uncommon one; it's certainly true that my mother, caught in the swirl of discourses as we all are, has picked up the notion of teachers birthed from the ether as well as from the culture. This doesn't mean, as we know, that this idea isn't also unique to her in the ways in which she espouses and adheres to it. I write the story here, however, because I think it's important to tease out, just a bit more, to take account of the many myths of the profession imposed from the outside just as they spring up, weedlike, in the cracks of our own winding disciplinary pathway. If, as is often suggested, teaching is a vocation, it is, also, something that cannot be taught. This is, perhaps, some of how we might take up Britzman's assertion, from Freud, that teaching is an impossible profession. I suspect, however, there's something different to it in the way I'm thinking of it here. No one is suggesting, in conversation with my friends who are accountants, that they were born to be accountants. Similarly, no one is telling them in casual conversation that, really, anyone could manage the tax situations of major corporations if they wanted to. And yet I'm reminded of a conversation with a friend who, in speaking of the teachers of their child who has profound special needs: "Really, anybody could teach if they wanted to. It doesn't really take any kind of unique skills," he said to me—a teacher educator.

But let's leave the gall aside for a second from this friend who owns an envelope-making company (which he inherited, so perhaps he was born to do it after all). Instead, I think we need to deal with the appearance of duality here: Only people who are born to teach can teach, and anyone could teach if they wanted to. My sense is that these actually aren't as much in tension as first appears because they are both tied up in the notion that teaching is linked to identity primarily. In the first idea, learning to teach is largely pointless as ontology matters most; in the second idea, learning to teach is largely pointless as ontology matters most; you are born a teacher because anyone could be born a teacher. And to close the loop on the tautology, anyone who ends up teaching was born to do it; anyone who never teaches or leaves teaching just wasn't born to do it. There's actually some hope in this slushed reading I'm doing, I think, but what can get sloughed off, then, is the notion that teacher identity matters in a fixed sense. This emerges from Adam's earlier reading clearly, but ultimately, teacher identity is intrinsically malleable because everyone is born to teach because anyone can teach; we just need to reconcile ourselves to the decision to do so and then learn how to move forward.

Adam: So, we move in this chapter to think broadly about "teacher identity" and how conversations about becoming a teacher are complicated by other aspects or parts of our identities. Central to this is contemplating the work of reconciliation and how we become not only reconciled to uncertainties in teaching but also reconcile identities that some may see as, because they may very well be, contradictory. We might remember, as Walt Whitman (1855/2005) asks in his "Song of Myself":

> Do I contradict myself?
> Very well then I contradict myself,
> (I am large, I contain multitudes)

Given this, how do we reconcile these contradictions, these multitudes we contain, as we become teachers? As we teach students becoming teachers?

Introduction

Part of becoming and being a teacher is having conversations with one's colleagues about the stuff that happens within a classroom. While teaching is, in general, a rather isolating profession, the isolation ends as colleagues converse about the workaday moments of the classroom. These conversations, at times, may be to sound a complaint or to brag of a success or to ask for guidance. Each type of conversation, we find, has value for a teacher's ever-evolving sense of identity. Additionally, each conversation, no matter the "type" is an embodied conversation that implicates teachers as racial, gendered, classed just as it does their ability, status, and sexual orientation. These conversations, in their everydayness, not only reveal the challenges that teachers can face around "identities" but also assist in coming to know a self. Indeed, Britzman (1993) argues that "as each of us struggles in the process of coming to know, we struggle not as autonomous beings who single-handedly perform singular feats, but as vulnerable social subjects who produce and are being produced by culture" (p. 28). Hers is a poststructural account of teacher identity, one that recognizes that our identity comes through the process of not only being subjected to discourses but also being a subject who speaks and acts. In becoming a subject who can claim an identity (or, more likely, identities), we encounter others who impact that process, making us both social and vulnerable. We are vulnerable to the ways others might identify us and in doing so draw on legacies of discourses that functioned to exclude and violate. And for teachers with marginalized identities, this challenge becomes fraught, something we want to explore in this chapter around LGBTQ+ and religious teachers. We focus on these identities because of, as we have shown throughout this book, the ways LGBTQ+ discourses and religious discourses often come head-to-head in the everyday moments of schools in which things are said and done. Such conversations, we believe, provide concrete incidents from which to make sense and perhaps develop personal theories about teaching and learning with others.

Theory, however, is rarely lauded by teachers given the ways in which theory, quite often, abstracts and idealizes. As Jane Gallop (2002), a theorist herself notes,

> Theory likes to set up an ideal realm where it need encounter no obstacle to the expansion of its understanding. By bracketing the incidents and situations in which it finds itself, theory can feel the exhilarating power to think untrammeled by feeling, life, and context. (p. 15)

Such a form of theory—unobstructed and bracketed—may be interesting to read, but within the rigamarole of a classroom, theory's abstractions, while potentially informative, can appear less helpful. We note this, however, not to disparage theory and its helpfulness. Rather, it is to recognize the importance of rethinking theory itself. For Gallop (2002), such rethinking meant recognizing theory's anecdotal formation. Theory, while it may like to disguise itself, is rooted in anecdotes, in incidents. Gallop argues as such, writing,

> Anecdotal theory drags theory into a scene where it must struggle for mastery. Theorizing in explicit relations to the here and now, theorizing because the subject feels the need to, theory must contend with what threatens its mastery. Subjecting theory to incident teaches us to think in precisely those situations which tend to disable thought, forces us to keep thinking even then the dominance of our thought is far from assured. (p. 15)

For teachers, anecdotal theory may align more closely with the ways in which they develop theories about teaching and learning and all the work both terms entail. Teachers need to theorize and do so amid incidents that disrupt, if only momentarily, a sense of mastery. Of particular interest in this chapter are the ways in which teachers theorize identity and the conflicts that emerge in such work. Such work is, as we explore, never singular but implicated in a variety of histories and politics that have framed the work of teachers and their "professionalism."

For teacher educators and student teachers in the 2020s, the discourses, strategies, and pedagogies to "master" have changed from previous generations, as is always the case with the ever-evolving realities of education and its stakeholders. We sense within these contexts that many teacher educators and student teachers are interested and often vested in various discourses, strategies, and pedagogies that engage the work of justice in education. We are vested in discourses, strategies, and pedagogies rooted in feminist, queer, and related "critical" theories, recognizing that within any given one of these there are important debates and tensions both "theoretically" and "materially." These tensions are not so much to be overcome but to be wrestled with as one encounters the everyday of education in relation to others coming into their own sense of "teacher" as well.

In the process of becoming a teacher, student teachers encounter a range of course work that can cause one to feel pushed and pulled in different directions or simply to become unsure of the relevance of such course work. This is, in our experience, often the case for "foundations of education" course work that seeks to bring students into historical and philosophical conversations and debates in education. Often, such course work, when still present, can be engaged in a rather dry manner, not allowing students to think through, for instance, how histories of American public education condition what is possible and impossible for them as educators. Historical discourses, put differently, both subject us to our pasts and allow us as subjects to intervene within the ways those pasts continue to impact our present. Such work, we believe, is central to developing a teacher identity as it conditions how we see which identities are feasible or possible.

The feasibility of identities is impacted by a range of factors, including the historic realities that schools, as socializing agents, have sought to cultivate particular types of subjects. And this cultivation has been for decades now challenged for the ways in which it subjects teachers to normalizing discourses. We might think here of the range of pedagogies that teacher education has on offer that have expanded pedagogical thought to include the previously excluded. We think about "deficit" pedagogies that were challenged, importantly by "culturally relevant pedagogies" (Ladson-Billings, 1995, 2014), which have themselves been "lovingly critiqued" to advocate for "culturally sustaining pedagogies" (Paris & Alim, 2014). This history alludes to, in part, the changing identities of teachers and their students' needs. We might, as well, look at pedagogies rooted in particular theories such as "feminist pedagogy" (Berry, 2010; hooks, 2000; Shrewsbury, 1989), "critical pedagogy" (Freire, 1970/2000; Giroux, 1988; Giroux & McLaren, 1989), "queer pedagogy" (Britzman, 1993; Luhmann, 1998), or "indigenous pedagogy" (Grande, 2004) that centralize the practices, histories, and identities of different communities that have fraught histories in and in relation to public education. In their various ways, these pedagogies open up opportunities to establish different teacher identities, even as they are limited and conditioned by the material realities of schools and their often deeply conservative social function.

Such schools of pedagogical thought are rooted within "research" with a sincere hope that research informs practice. After all, the research that informs these pedagogical schools emerges itself from forms of practice whether that is a particular type of research practice or research on teaching practices. Our interest in noting this is not in reifying a "research/practice" or "theory/practice" divide; rather, we are interested instead in thinking carefully about the different albeit related projects in play as student teachers and teacher educators encounter them together. As we explored earlier, student teachers and teacher educators are tasked with "considering everything" such that in considering everything, one becomes, hopefully, more considerate. One also engages in the process of becoming a subject. We cannot, of course, ever consider everything since the things that we must consider inevitably change. Rather, the process of considering asks that we take seriously the diverse work at hand, including the reality that education as a "field" must consider diverse disciplines that can, at first glance, be rather overwhelming.

Such considerations are, we want to suggest here, implicated in the work of becoming a teacher. "Becoming" here is used intentionally to think about the ways in which, as subjects, we are always in the process of becoming subjects. For Foucault, there was a certain poetics to the term *subject* given the different ways in which the word operates. We are subjects who can take the place of the "subject position" in a sentence. We are the subjects that write, that teach, that make decisions. We are, as well, subject to particular discourses, norms, and technologies that discipline, surveil, reward, and punish. And within schools, we encounter various school subjects that we are subjected to day in and day out but that simultaneously assist us in becoming subjects—knowledgeable subjects, perhaps. Within the scenes of teacher education then, teacher educators subject student teachers to particular discourses, norms, and technologies with a goal, in part, of helping students become teachers of particular subjects or "content areas." Yet, such a process is neither simple nor straightforward as even amid "critical" discourses, there remain the threats of normalization and discipline.

Given this, as Britzman (2007) argues, our development as teachers is uncertain perhaps even more so as we become more attentive to the workings of power and the expanding ways schools are conceived and perceived in the public.

Such a poetic play with subject may, for some readers, be a bit overwrought. *Subject, subjectivity,* and *subjectivization* are terms that are prominently used within certain poststructural discourses. They are, often enough, dismissed as jargon. And poststructural discourses are far from the norm in most teacher education programs given the ways in which the field is rooted in certain positivist or postpositivist discourses. Additionally, teacher education is to some extent, by definition, interested in looking ahead and assisting student teachers in developing practices and "teacher identities" for their future. Poststructuralism, on the other hand, more often than not looks backward at the ways discourses and related practices have "come to be," an insight from Cleo Cherryholmes (1999), who was not opposed to poststructural thought but helped distinguish its form of "reading" from other forms of reading, like those of feminism and pragmatism.

Reading, here, is fundamental but complicated since we never read from some neutral point of view but, rather, read from our own subject positions. Yet our own subject positions do not arise naturally but come through our own experiences being subjected to "this" practice or idea or concept instead of "that" practice or idea or concept. And combined and changing, these experiences impact how we come to identify and see ourselves in relation to others.

This causes us to think about the contingency of becoming a teacher given the ways we become a teacher in a particular time and place in which we have access to some discourses, ideas, or practices and not others. And while we might bring new or different ideas to the pedagogical conversations that emerge from this limited reality, those conversations are still largely bound by context. This is not to imply that such scenes are always already determined but to recognize the myriad decisions that are made within an educational scene that can lead to various consequences. Again, affirming our lesson from Phyllis's understanding of ethics, it has two parts—always questioning what we think is good and doing less harm next time (Fendler, 2011).

So what are we getting at here? Well, we are getting at historical complexities alongside the present circumstances of teacher identity. We can look historically to see how teacher identity has been framed and often limited by schools. This is visible when we look at the relationship between teaching and morality that has, in particular, impacted not only gay and lesbian teachers subjected to "morality clauses" but also single female teachers who, for a time, were viewed as potentially cultivating spinster students (Blount, 2000, 2006). This historical turn helps us think about the ways racialized people have been excluded from the teaching profession just as it raises concerns around the barriers to full participation placed in the way of teachers with disabilities. Put differently, minoritized subjects have encountered a rather unrelenting task of trying to "fit" into the teaching profession just as in doing so they have expanded publicly acceptable notions of who is fit to teach. Research on teacher identity has often focused on particular subjects while, at the same time, recognizing the ways in which those subjects are themselves complicated (Jenlink, 2020). We attend to particular complications around sexuality and religion in this chapter.

A common concern when it comes to minoritized identity in the teaching force is that such an identity subjects students, perceived often as in need of protection, to "strange" ideas disrupting various norms and dominant ideologies. Schools as socializing agents are held in special regard for the ways in which they are perceived to influence and inform how students become subjects themselves. In practice, this opens up any range of paradoxes and challenges regarding what is taught and who teaches it. Recognizing this, we want to shift to think through teacher-identity research. We do this first by turning to the conceptual landscape that informs our thinking, namely, poststructural investigations of "identity." Following this, we turn to anthropological and sociological research on LGBTQ+ and religious teachers. In doing so, we seek to bring together two "types" of teachers to illustrate what may be common concerns from very different positions.

Identity to Subject

Our turn, in this chapter, to teacher identity might easily be seen as a turn to "identity politics." Identity politics, as a discourse, is one that is often pilloried, just as it's caricatured, for its limitations. For instance, identity politics by some accounts is viewed as developing separatist politics that focus on a particular identity at the expense of other possible political frames. We are uninterested in rehashing these debates—both from the 1980s and 1990s and, more recently, after the 2016 U.S. presidential election. Rather, we would prefer to recognize that politics always implicates our identities, and our identities are never singular. We engage in identity politics, by definition, since we cannot be divorced from our identities. Yet, in writing this, we recognize that our identities are more often than not complicated and contradictory leading to moments in which one might be accused of working against one's own interests. These complications and their attendant contradictions impact our own emotional lives (how can I be "x" and "y" or, perhaps more likely, how can they be both "a" and "b") and are often informed by our relations with others and broader political, cultural, and historical realities. We can identify in a number of ways but how we identify can be contested by how others identify us. Within schools, this becomes fraught as identities can become the fodder of rumors and scandals that have material consequences—a reality played out in communities and court cases (see *Morrison v State Board of Education*, 1969).

Identity politics, as such, becomes a necessity both to engage in and critique. This is, for us, a key lesson from early queer scholarship given the ways in those early years queer theorists were criticized for supposedly depoliticizing identity. Judith Butler (1993), in "Critically Queer," challenges such criticisms, offering a genealogical critique of the queer subject: "The queer subject," Butler argues, "will be central to queer politics to the extent that it constitutes a self-critical dimension within activism, a persistent reminder to take the time to consider the exclusionary force of one of activism's most treasured contemporary premises" (p 19). Identity, a queer identity in Butler's sense, is not merely done away with magically by poststructural critiques. Rather, critiques of identity are the stuff that holds open the ways in which identities alongside discourses and power relations constitute subjects. Or, to draw on Butler again,

> as much as identity terms must be used, as much as 'outness' is to
> be affirmed, these same notions must become subject to a critique
> of the exclusionary operations of their own production: for whom
> is outness an historically available and affordable option? (p. 19)

Of course, the key lesson of intersectionality (Crenshaw, 1989) is that identity—and its baggage—is never singular but wrapped up with how one identity overlaps with other identities and their attendant material conditions.

Outness, in Butler's statement, is never without critique given that there are costs to being out that some simply may not be able to bear. This reality is evident, as we discuss later, within the histories of LGBTQ+ teachers given the prominence of the "closet" in sexuality and gender politics. But it will also be visible within the ways the "closet" as a discourse has traveled elsewhere, allowing others to express challenges of "being out" (especially in certain spaces in higher education) as, for instance, an Evangelical Christian.

With Butler's Foucauldian-informed lesson on the dual necessity of, and necessity of critiquing, identity politics we turn to think through how such lessons play out more specifically within teacher identity research. This is not, mind you, to necessarily add to teacher-identity research through an empirical study but to contemplate the ways the different research on "teacher identity" has use value to draw together the challenges that face LGBTQ+ and religious teachers. Or, perhaps put differently, we look to teacher-identity research on LGBTQ+ teachers and religious teachers[1] to draw insights on their different and common challenges. We sense, at the outset, that their common challenges have to do with the shared realities of becoming a teacher. Becoming a teacher is difficult and uncertain. Their differences, however, we sense, come in the ways LGBTQ+ rhetorics and religious rhetorics contest or complicate one another.

Recruiting Queers

"Do you approve of legislation allowing known practicing homosexuals to teach in public, private, and religious schools?" This was the first question Anita Bryant asked in the "Official Public Opinion Survey" ballot that she sent out to her supporters. With this question and Bryant's larger Save Our Children Campaign, we see the emergence of a recurring fear that persists: the fear that queers recruit and often in schools. Bryant's Save Our Children Campaign, along with California's Briggs Initiative in the 1970s, captured a backlash against the rise of gay rights discourses, with each of these related initiatives seeking to show how gay rights ordinances and "radical militant homosexuals" would harm children. As Bryant (1977) wrote in her newsletter, "I don't hate homosexuals! But as a mother, I must protect my children from their evil influence," which she later notes was, in part, that "they want to recruit your children and teach them the virtues of becoming a homosexual." Such lessons, she feared would allow homosexuality to be seen as "an alternative lifestyle" (p. 103). Bryant felt she could not remain silent as the then "emerging" homosexuals sought to "claim they are a legitimate minority group." Such claims, she asserted, needed to be challenged in the name of love.

The legacies of Bryant's campaign are complicated given the ways her early successes in repealing antidiscrimination ordinances protecting homosexuals were quickly overturned. And while that was the case, her campaigns contributed to a certain mainstreaming of religiously informed arguments against "homosexual teachers." This existed alongside queer reclamations of the "recruitment fear," heard, for instance, during Harvey Milk's campaign in which he would famously note, "I'm here to recruit you!" This fear of recruitment, however, becomes charged when LGBTQ+ teachers are engaged in conversations about teaching as they quite frequently cite this fear as a reason for not being out or to signal their hesitancy in bringing LGBTQ+ issues into their curriculum. The homophobic fear of recruitment that LGBTQ+ teachers have been subjected to becomes, in such moments, a part of their psychic and embodied experiences of teaching.

Catherine Connell (2015) in *School's Out: Gay and Lesbian Teachers in the Classroom,* documents the complex ways in which lesbian and gay teachers in California and Texas navigate their teacher identity. Gay and lesbian teachers, she argues, "are doubly constrained, on the one hand by the norms of teaching professionalism and on the other by the identity demands of the gay rights movement" (p. 5). Through her research and interviews with her participants, she found that generally teachers managed this dialectic between pride and professionalism utilizing one of three strategies: splitting, knitting, or quitting. She found that there were teachers who split their sexual identity from their teacher identity, maintaining private and public personas; teachers who knit their sexual identity and teacher identity together; and those who quit the teaching profession altogether. The decisions of teachers to "split, knit, or quit" were rooted in their own contexts and communities. The rights of LGBTQ+ teachers and students are themselves contextual given the tapestry of human rights ordinances, state laws, and with the *Bostock* (2020) decision, federal protections for employees based on sexual and gender identity. What Connell's work documented, however, are the ways in which lesbian and gay teachers navigate on-the-ground realities in which the abstractions of "pride" and "professionalism" come to life.

Pride and professionalism, to stay with Connell's (2015) dialectic, are no joke as they come to impact the material practices and lives of teachers. These rhetorics rooted in their own histories, come head-to-head with myriad consequences for teachers who, in their contexts and communities, might fail to cultivate an "identity" that merges them successfully. These failures might be seen as such by queer teachers who, for instance, may want to be "out" in a way they think or feel they cannot be. But such failures may as well be a projection onto queer teachers with expectations of what or how "queer" teachers should act. Connell's findings on how teachers manage this—splitting, knitting, or quitting—emerge from her conversations with teachers. These teachers have within their contexts found ways to "be" in classrooms. Yet, to outsiders looking in, any particular management strategy may be seen as a failure to either be a "good queer role model" or a "good public school teacher," depending on the rhetorics that one privileges. One of Connell's arguments is that "teachers will not be able to reconcile their political and professional selves until we systematically challenge the ideology that upholds the tensions between pride and professionalism" (p. 5). Reconciliation rears its head here, but what exactly is meant by reconciliation? This is something we explore shortly after grounding ourselves further in the issues that exist around LGBTQ+ teachers and religious teachers.

As we have noted at various points already, a key challenge for LGBTQ+ subjects has been the way teachers were constructed—through political, religious, and legal arguments—and how that construction was at odds with the ways LGBTQ+ subjects have been constructed—as deviant, pathological, immoral. While discourses around LGBTQ+ subjects have evolved, the legacies of deviancy, pathology, and immorality persist, in part, we would note, because of the intergenerational reality of schools. Teachers develop their "teacher identity" rooted in time and place. These times and places are not just related to pedagogical and instructional strategies but also, in larger ways, to how teaching and teachers are perceived. In this time and place, one comes into a sense of "teacher identity" that is not deterministic of their identity, allowing for the ways in which identity can change, providing initial frameworks that can be challenging to counter or unlearn. These challenges become more visible as teachers encounter the changing student body and their identities, which affirm the importance of hospitality.

Evangelizing Evangelicals

While there is a fear of recruitment on the part of LGBTQ+ teachers, a similar fear emerges around religious teachers. This, notably, comes from a concern that religious teachers will evangelize students. This fear is likely most salient in recent examinations of state voucher systems, which have given substantial public funding to schools that teach Young Earth Creationism (Gaddy, 2013) but extends historically to battles over the imposition of Protestant prayer and Bibles on Catholics (DelFattore, 2004; Dolan, 2002) and further to more broad-based critiques of Christian privilege and the desire to convert that remains rooted in the DNA of U.S. public education (e.g., Blumenfeld et al., 2009; Burke & Segall, 2017) even in its secularized-religious form. This last critique asserts that the very structures of American public education are steeped in Christianity and that only recently in its history has religion become contested (as visible, for instance, in the history of Supreme Court decisions). As such, evangelization of a particular bent is endemic to the educational project in the United States.

Hadley (2021), in her study of evangelical teachers, finds evidence of this effect. In a parallel to Connell's (2015) study, we see a similar tension between the rhetoric of professionalism and the rhetoric of evangelical Christianity. However, unlike the fear of recruitment used against LGBTQ+ teachers, even though recruitment is a myth (or a queer parody of straight fears), Hadley showed how, for some evangelical teachers, the fear of evangelizing is one rooted in the deep existential disappointment that one has failed.

For instance, Mallory, one of Hadley's (2021) participants, describes religion as "the family business"; indeed, her father is "one of the founders of a local megachurch; her mother taught at Christian private schools" (p. 122). Her brother is "a recent graduate from a very conservative seminary" (p. 122) and she has, since publication of the book, married a graduate from a more liberal Christian seminary. Largely due to this background, Mallory "felt spiritually called to the work" of teaching (p. 125). She has, however, developed an ambivalence toward the religion of her family most especially regarding rhetoric about love and the treatment of LGBTQ+ students. She notes that love in her family's church mostly meant "correcting others," which feels disconnected from how she demonstrates care to her students, saying, "'I don't think there's a way to "correct" LGBTQ+ students without them feeling rejected, and I see a disconnect in those two things. For me, the way I made peace with that is that I am gay-affirming'" (p. 128).

We bring forward Mallory's example not to discount the very real discourses around conversion that may often drive religious teachers in public schools. Rather, we want to suggest that there is a complication here, and dismissing Mallory's religion or perhaps dismissing Mallory for our perceptions of her religiosity (she very much projects "religious" vibes even in the clothing she wears, as Hadley, 2021, documented) in teacher education courses misses the ways in which her own internal shifts may, in fact, come to drive a more progressive approach to affirming gay students. Hadley's ability to speak the idiom of religious discourse allows her access to some of the turmoil that movement from conservative to progressive religious views causes a beginning teacher like Mallory. We need to understand this shift better as there may be push points accessible to teacher education if we look closely.

There are hints, as well, in Olshefski's (2020) work, which offers an account of "the religious beliefs and experiences of a white Evangelical English teacher" and how her enthusiastic embrace of "anti-racist pedagogy" was tempered by her struggle in "embracing LGBTQ+ advocacy" (p. 1). Olshefski sits with the difficulties of a young teacher making sense of the limits of her commitments to justice. The easy, and perhaps viscerally satisfying, answer is simply that this person, and people like her, shouldn't be in schools, let alone around LGBTQ+ students. That their attempts to "love" their students out of their sin will only cause damage and strife. And on that latter point, we're wholly sympathetic. On the former, however, we need to attend to the reality of the teacher workforce in the United States: It is, as noted earlier, disproportionately religious (and White and female). And if multicultural and critical education, as we have approached them in the last 30-odd years in the field of teacher education, still produce these dilemmas in teachers, then we're failing at our task not only of protecting LGBTQ+ students but also of preparing real, actual teachers as they exist to work in classrooms in ways that we see as just and affirming.

We might hope that Amy, as she is called in the article, somehow becomes Mallory through a process of conversion, that the scales fall away from her eyes. But we really don't know how to affect something like that. And in any event, aren't we just indulging our own conversion fantasies in a different way? As we seek ways forward, we would do well to sit with the data as they exist—and sparse as they are—to find a way or many ways forward in teacher education. As she thinks about her views, Amy cites "The Nashville Statement" (NS), a document from 2017 that emerged from the Southern Baptist Convention (SBC). The SBC is the largest Protestant denomination in the United States, and so it is, of course, significant that the NS states that "homosexual immorality or transgenderism . . . constitute an essential departure from Christian faithfulness and witness" (p. 3). Amy's interpretation of this is that the "Bible's position was 'pretty clear' that homosexuality was 'not ok'" (Olshefski, 2021, p. 11). Leaving aside, for a moment, that the Bible is, in fact, pretty ambiguous on the topic such as it is or was understood across the time period when various texts were being compiled into the books of the Bible (e.g., Cahill, 1996; Farley, 2006; Salzman & Lawler, 2008), we can turn to think with Olshefski (2021) about what this means for teacher education. He notes that "some, if not most, readers are bound to question Amy's suitability as a . . . teacher" (p. 12). And although this might, in fact, become what a reasonable reader decides in this particular case, we have to understand that Amy is likely not particularly unique in the teaching ranks. Olshefski suggests that "teacher educators need to take care to handle" (p. 13) affirmation of LGBTQ+ positions *in relation to* religious teachers' concerns. And while this is, in a sense, bowing to majoritarian impulses—why must we always respond to the needs of the privileged?—we also have to acknowledge that in many places, these concerns for teacher candidates exist but are largely at the level of an undercurrent in the classroom. Amy notes that when issues of LGBTQ+ affirmation come up, she tends to "err on the side of quiet" (p. 13), something Thein (2013) has found in the past. The point of this book is that actively addressing the issue does not allow that quietude to fester into a sense of persecution. And so, with Olshefski, our stance is, and continues to be, that we can offer different authoritative texts, in the idiom of religion and through theology, that stand up next to the NS and its coadjutors. We could begin with Merton's (1965) response to the dangers of propaganda, and specifically religious propaganda as earlier, noting that "propaganda *makes up our mind* for us" (p. 238, emphasis in original) such that we forget that "the more we insist" on making religion merely about "the avoidance of sin (especially in the realm of sex) . . . the more we make faith into a mental and spiritual problem, contingent on a certain ethical achievement" (p. 167). This is in contrast to a living religion that meets individuals in their needs and desires as they are rather than as they might be dehumanized into. We might better ask, as Goss (1998) does, how we can "create a Christianity that escapes from its heritage of violence and from its irrelevancy in addressing the spiritual needs of gays/lesbians" (p. 192). Farley (2006) notes that the "experience of sex combines embodied love and desire, conversation and communication ... transcendence into fuller selves, and even encounter with God" such that "these human possibilities need not be limited by culturally constructed boundaries of gender" (p. 173). Here the language of the transcendent gives us access to a different patios for speaking about sexual and gender multiplicity. Shifting a religious, and particularly a White Christian sense of how to attend to the spiritual needs of LGBTQ+ individuals will necessitate engagement with religious texts, theological ones, and it will require a return to the hermeneutical. Shying away from theology means that Amy's sense of the Bible stands without nuance or challenge and its attendant discourses about the proper treatment of LGBTQ+ issues and students never are held up to the light for inspection in teacher education.

Indoctrination

Whether "queer" or "evangelical," teachers for whom identities collide, we notice shared challenges in becoming. Queer teachers struggle between rhetorics of pride and professionalism while evangelical teachers struggle between rhetorics of Evangelism and professionalism. Such struggles document the very real ways that education continues to be seen as a site of potential indoctrination. Queers potentially indoctrinate through recruitment; evangelicals potentially indoctrinate through religious proselytization. The reality seems to be more complicated as the stories of teachers illustrate sincere struggles with the responsibilities of being a public employee and a private citizen and, for evangelicals, a faithful servant. Politically, it seems more newsworthy to find cases in which this may not be the case, where teachers cross lines (real or imagined). Yet what we want to get at here is that within teacher education there is a real need to wrestle with these questions as they emerge, this so that abstract commitments to things like equality, freedom, and expression are turned into pedagogical practices that do less harm to new generations amid their own becoming. To do so, we suggest a turn to reconciliation.

Reconciling Selves

As noted earlier, Connell (2015) argues for the need for teachers to reconcile parts of one's self that are in tension with one another. For her, lesbian and gay teachers (and we can broaden that to include other forms of queer identity) need to find ways to reconcile their political and professional selves. In a related way, evangelical teachers (and we can broaden that to include other forms of religious identity) also have to find ways to reconcile their religious beliefs with their role as public servants. Yet what is left underdeveloped is the work of reconciliation itself. What might it mean to "reconcile" selves? To think through this, we turn to theology and its understandings of reconciliation.

Reconciliation is, within the Catholic Church, a sacrament. Theologically, it has come to encompass the ritual practice in which a sinner confesses sins and, upon confession, is provided absolution by a priest. This absolution is, broadly speaking, conditional on the performance of penance that has become, as noted in the previous chapter, rather perfunctory in many cases, something like a coach yelling, "Drop and give me 20," whereby push-ups are replaced by rote prayer. That's a bit of a caricature, of course, but the point is that much has changed in the relationship between penance and reconciliation over time in the church. This is useful, we hope, for helping us think about the possibilities for reconciling as a practice in teacher education as it wrestles with questions of teacher identity.

Foucault (2014) makes the point that in the early church, "penance was a status . . . that embraced all aspects of one's existence" (p. 105), and although that status could be sought or imposed, it was only abjured through the act of veridiction (verbal avowal of one's sinfulness) and the ritual, originally on Good Friday, whereupon reconciliation for one's sins was granted. We don't need to go further into Foucault's account here, as what we have is already useful enough. There are concatenations of this ancient practice, updated for modern times, run throughout our conceptualizations of the role of students and teachers and schooling in general. Certainly there are parallels to the ways in which punishment is wrought in schools (detention in which one remains a penitent until released and reconciled at the end of a given period of time), but what we find most interesting for our purposes is the possibility and danger of the moment of reconciliation. For it is imbued with power.

To reconcile tensions, we suggest might sound generative on its face, but may on closer inspection cover up the necessity of tensions and struggle. In Foucault's account and in the ways in which such a concept might be considered facilely in schools, we can think about how teachers have, over the years, demanded a kind of penitent status be imposed on students, just as the narrative seems to suggest a shift whereby students are increasingly demanding penance from teachers for their sins of being, for instance, not only not woke enough, but also too flamboyant or devotional. The trouble with living in this space, however, is it allows for a kind of weaponization of forgiveness as "a particularly clever form of vengeance" (Alison, 2001, p. 33), whereby forgiveness emerges in a relationship of "sanctimonious weakness" that requires a victim seeking to be forgiven in parasitical relationship with "the brute power which has to have forgiveness helplessly pronounced at it" (p. 34).

We can see the roots here of popular constructions that begin with "I'm not going to apologize for x anymore." In many cases, we see this claimed about Whiteness; in others, religion; in prior instantiations, this was much used by LGBTQ+ individuals. The power imbalances of those three groups, even as they overlap in their identities, are clear, but our point is that a system rooted in the demand for forgiveness keeps everyone a penitent in search of the ultimate arbiter of reconciliation: We're seeking a ritual for forgiveness while forgetting our role in upholding its impossibility—or, rather, its cyclicality, a tautology of repetition. Margaret Farley (2006) suggests two ways to escape this ouroboric situation in educational spaces: relationship and intimacy. She notes that, from a theological standpoint, "when we open to relationship through knowledge and love, we transcend what we already are. To step into relation with another is to step out of a center that holds only ourselves" (p. 129). This relationality only works, however, if we acknowledge and honor the intimacy that emerges from and through our bodies:

> We are gifted in body and spirit by all creation's speaking to us
> God's word and providing us a home where we may find sustenance
> and joy. We embody ourselves in intimate relationships with one
> another, and in less intimate still bodily relationships with many
> others in societies where our dwellings extend our skins and we
> learn to thirst not only in body but in spirit. (p. 117)

Salzman and Lawler (2008) suggest that, in specific relation to bodily engagement, "sexual intercourse is reconciling" because it "affirms self, other, and the relationship through healing and reconciliation" (p. 133). This is not, to be clear, a call for wonton sexual engagement in schools. What we want to suggest, however, is that our engagement with the irreconcilable tension of hospitality of "who or what shows up" will necessarily mean thinking with and about the religious orientations and entanglements of our teacher education students (just as we engage with our own) in similar, although different, ways in which we have to do the same work thinking about the sexual orientations and gender identities of our teacher education students (and our own). Such work, we think, must be done if we are to take seriously the necessity of welcoming students and selves amid their conflicting identities.

Given the relationship between reconciliation and forgiveness, let us be clear. This isn't a call to forgive religion its sins—most especially as we see the deadly effects of White nationalist Christianity weaponized over time and most recently against democratic governance. It is, rather, a call to realize that we are in relationship with White Christianity and particularly White Christians within our classroom or in the broader engagement with the field of teacher education. Christianity, particularly White Christianity, has held a particular sway within public education that has contributed to the challenges faced by queer students and teachers alike. We cannot, however, dismiss Christianity, nor can we simply ask queers to forgive. We are also in relationship with other religious denominations and experiences in our classrooms, mostly considered in scholarship and practice in teacher education. What, then, must we do?

Perhaps the moment provides for returning to intercourse. Here we seek to recover the term from its sexual connotation—without removing the traces of such a modification as if that were ever possible. Indeed, immediately following a definition of "sexual connection" (Definition 2d) is listed a much older understanding of "communion between" individuals "which is spiritual or unseen" (Definition 3). This communion, this connection, only happens in the exchange of ideas inherent in an intercourse in teacher education. And one of the ways we find ourselves emerging from the ruts of incommensurability wrought of the culture wars is working to understand how to reconcile religious resistance to sexual progress and sexual plurality to the constraints of conservative Christianity especially. This is not to create closure, or reinforce the need for penance and forgiveness, whose power would become centrally located in an authority of one kind or another. We aren't seeking to re-create different gatekeepers here but, rather, to suggest that reconciliation, different from acceptance or surrender and more complex than tolerance or understanding, means coming to account for the tensions and aporias present in becoming a teacher and developing an identity. We further examine the production of these tensions in the next chapter, our conclusion, with an exploration of the usefulness and limitations of accompaniment in education.

Endnotes

1 This dichotomy is a problem that we need to acknowledge. Certainly there are religious teachers who also will identify in some way as LGBTQ+. We don't want to elide this overlap entirely but are adopting the traditional split in communities here to suggest that there are, in fact, overlaps that exist for teachers who would not generally span the gap, as it were.

References

Alison, J. (2001). *Faith beyond resentment: Fragments Catholic and gay.* Crossroad Publishing Group.

Berry, T. R. (2000, Summer/Fall). Engaged pedagogy and critical race feminism. *Educational Foundations*, 19–26.

Blount, J. (2000). Spinsters, bachelors, and other gender transgressors in school employment, 1850–1990. *Review of Educational Research*, 70(1), 83–101.

Blount, J. (2006). *Fit to teach: Same-sex desire, gender, and school work in the twentieth century.* SUNY Press.

Blumenfeld, W. J., Joshi, K. Y., & Fairchild, E. E. (Eds.). (2009). *Investigating Christian privilege and religious oppression in the United States.* Sense Publishers.

Bostock v. Clayton County, 140 S. Ct. 1731, 207 L. Ed. 2d 218 (2020).

Britzman, D. (1993). The terrible problem of knowing thyself: Toward a poststructural account of teacher identity. *Journal of Curriculum Theorizing*, 9(3), 23–46.

Britzman, D. (2007). Teacher education as uneven development: Towards a psychology of uncertainty. *International Journal of Leadership in Education*, 10(1), 1–12.

Bryant, A. (1977). *When the homosexuals burn the Holy Bible in Public… How can I stand by silently* [Newsletter]. Anita Bryant Ministries.

Burke, K. J., & Segall, A. (2017). *Christian privilege in US education: Legacies and current issues.* Routledge.

Butler, J. (1993). Critically queer. *GLQ*, 1(1), 17–32.

Cahill, L. S. (1996). *Sex, gender & Christian ethics.* Cambridge University Press.

Cherryholmes, C. (1999). *Reading pragmatism.* Teachers College Press.

Connell, C. (2015). *School's out: Gay and lesbian teachers in the classroom.* University of California Press.

Council of Biblical Manhood and Womanhood. (2017). *The Nashville statement.* https:// cbmw.org/nashville-statement/

Crenshaw, K. (1989). Demarginalizing the intersection of race and sex: A Black feminist critique of antidiscrimination doctrine, feminist theory, and antiracist politics. *The University of Chicago Legal Forum, 139,* 139–167.

DelFattore, J. (2004). *The fourth r: Conflicts over religion in America's public schools.* Yale University Press.

Dolan, J. (2002). *In search of an American Catholicism: A history of religion and culture in tension.* Oxford University Press.

Farley, M. (2006). *Just love: A framework for Christian sexual ethics.* Continuum.

Fendler, L. (2011). Edwin and Phyllis. *Studies in Philosophy and Education, 30*(5), 463–469.

Foucault, M. (2014). *Wrong-doing, truth-telling: The function of avowal in justice* (S. W. Sawyer, Trans.; F. Brion & B. E. Harcourt, Eds.). University of Chicago Press.

Freire, P. (2000). *Pedagogy of the oppressed.* Continuum. (Original work published 1970)

Gaddy, C. W. (2013, April 1). Creationism and taxes in Louisiana. *Washington Post.* https://www.washingtonpost.com/national/on-faith/creationism-and-taxes-in-louisiana/2013/04/01/be823746-9ae5-11e2-a941-a19bce7af755_story.html

Gallop, J. (2002). *Anecdotal theory.* Duke University Press.

Giroux, H. A. (1988). *Teachers as intellectuals: Toward a critical pedagogy of learning.* Bergin and Garvey Publishing.

Giroux, H. A., & McLaren, P. (Eds). (1989). *Critical pedagogy, the state, and cultural struggle.* SUNY Press.

Goss, R. E. (1998). Sexual visionaries and freedom fighters. In S. Gill (Ed.), *The lesbian and gay Christian movement: Campaigning for justice, truth, and love* (pp. 187–202). Continuum.

Grande, S. (2004). *Red pedagogy: Native American social and political thought.* Rowman & Littlefield.

Hadley, H. L. (2021). *Navigating moments of hesitation: Portraits of evangelical English language arts teachers.* Myers Education Press.

hooks, b. (2000). Feminist education for critical consciousness. In *Feminism is for everybody* (pp. 19–24). South End Press.

Jenlink, P. M. (Ed.). (2020). *Sexual orientation and teacher identity: Professionalism and LGBTQ politics in teacher preparation and practice.* Rowman & Littlefield.

Ladson-Billings, G. (1995). Toward a theory of culturally relevant pedagogy. *American Education Research Journal, 32*(3), 465–491.

Ladson-Billings, G. (2014). Culturally relevant pedagogy 2.0: a.k.a. the remix. *Harvard Educational Review, 84*(1), 74–84.

Luhmann, S. (1998). Queering/querying pedagogy? Or, pedagogy is a pretty queer thing. In W. Pinar (Ed.), *Queer theory in education* (pp. 120–132). Lawrence Erlbaum.

Merton, T. (1965). *Conjectures of a guilty bystander.* Image Book.

Morrison v State Board of Education. 461 P.2d 375 (1969).

Paris, D., & Alim, H. S. (2014). What are we seeking to sustain through culturally sustaining pedagogy? A loving critique forward. *Harvard Educational Review, 84*(1), 85–100.

Olshefski, C. (2021). Anti-racist, anti-gay: A White evangelical English teacher's negotiations of her faith and critical inquiry. *English Teaching: Practice and Critique.* Advanced online publication. https://doi.org/10.1108/ETPC-10-2019-0124

Salzman, T., & Lawler, M. (2008). *The sexual person: Toward a renewed Catholic anthropology.* Georgetown University Press.

Shrewsbury, C. M. (1987). What is feminist pedagogy? *Women's Studies Quarterly, 15*(3/4), 6–14.

Thein, A.H. (2013), "Language arts teachers' resistance to teaching LGBT literature and issues", Language Arts, Vol. 90 No. 3, pp. 169-180.

Whitman, W. (2005). Walt Whitman's Leaves of grass: The first (1855) edition. Penguin Books.

On Accompaniment

A Preliminary Conversation

Kevin: As we've wrote this book, we were also working on a special issue for the journal *Sex Education* around a similar set of questions. More or less, in that space, we tried to think with the brilliant Mary Lou Rasmussen about what it would mean for the field of sexuality education to move to the side of a model which sets progressive sexuality education against religion. In that scenario, the assumption, and not without some evidence it's worth saying, is that religion manifests itself in relation to sexuality and its public education *solely* in conservative strands of theological belief. Mary Lou's long written about how this is, in fact, largely untrue and that on the ground, well, things are more complicated. One of the papers that went into that issue, in fact, shows that youth across the religious spectrum (from atheists to believers) and from among a number of religious belief systems are deeply curious about religious beliefs as they relate to sexuality just as they are interested in learning sexuality education that responds to various understandings of sex and gender in the world (Sell & Reiss, 2021). One lesson, I suppose is, well, the kids are all right. But another is that adults in charge of the curriculum are often preternaturally timid. Alison (2003), in his examination of accompaniment—my favorite of his themes— suggests that gay Catholics would do well to understand that God asks, "What would it be fun to present to our [God] on his return?" (p. 112), suggesting that one way to interpret this question is to assume that "the author of all things speaks into being a daring conscience" (p. 113).

I don't want to suggest that what we've done here is at all daring. It's not. It's a book we had the privilege to write remotely together in the middle of terribly real global catastrophes. But as we close the book, what I hope emerges is this sense that we have been curious to accompany each other through the journey of the work. Much of that is hidden to the reader, clearly, but it's the curiosity

and the gentleness of the encounter that characterize accompaniment. We distinguish this from a more relentless and juridical sense of accommodation in
the chapter as we close, but the central lesson, I think, is that we can find accompaniment along the way as teacher educators through a number of theories
in service of our students and their students. That accompaniment, the rhythm
underneath the melody of our teaching, will likely be enlivened by different
understandings of religious discourses even if the effect is the dissonance that
emerges from a clash of feedback. That's music too.

Adam: What is hidden and perhaps central to thinking about accompaniment is the role of time. Time is not only ever present and ever moving but also
quite strange as we experience it. We can, sticking with music, lose track of time
amid scenes of ecstatic dancing. I think here of years of going to gay clubs, music
thumping, sweaty bodies touching, as hours pass by in a blur. It is for me, the closest thing to a religious experience, an often weekly ritual akin to church, where
bodies meet to give praise and worship to some unseen but deeply felt connection
to histories that preceded us. That time within that space provides a momentary
reprieve from the outside world while simultaneously reproducing some of the
problematic dynamics of that same world. Yet we dance, music blaring, losing
track of time while finding ourselves amid strangers who may, in time, become
lovers or friends or one-night stands or nothing but a glance once, sidelong in the
dark. My turn to the gay bar and its times is intentional in thinking through not
so much the space itself but the time shared in those spaces with others who are,
in related but differing ways, coming into queer presence. There is for me a form
of accompaniment made possible during that time as, in the best-case scenarios,
queers recognize that the journey and process of "coming out" are unique and
cannot be forced. There is a temporal component to "becoming queer" that is not
only precarious but also rooted in embodied histories.

For me, as we have worked through and written this book, the role of time
has become more and more important. This is not only the time it takes to write
collaboratively, or the time it takes to work through defensive responses to the
work itself, but also the time it takes to encounter others in scenes of education that are at the heart of this project. Education is, of course, different from
school. Schooltime, I like to remind my students, is not the same as the time of
education. And often, education, when it does happen in schooltime, emerges
in moments of difficulty or controversy or scandal. These moments can often

erupt onto media landscapes in ways that may oversimplify or make villains of parties involved. Such moments, it seems, more often than not, are resolved through quick solutions (a fired teacher, a student removed from campus). A different approach would require staying with the trouble, lingering in its midst, finding time to work through its entanglements. It is the work of staying with the trouble that, for me, captures a key component of accompaniment. Accompaniment is a temporal relationship to others rooted, as we have attempted to argue here, in liking the other. Accompaniment, alongside the other, recognizes the role of time in helping the other (and the self) to come into presence in the ongoing work of becoming a subject. This accompaniment, as we explore in the chapter, does not predetermine the destination, which may sound weak. But as we explore, weakness may be a needed thing when encountering the tensions and possibilities as religion, sexuality, and gender meet in classrooms in diverse contexts and communities in different times.

Kevin: I get really antsy with aphoristic educational models. This is a product of my own teacher education program—an alternative certification path for Catholic school teachers—as well as with my role in my first job out of the doctorate working for that same program as a faculty member. But it's also a product of the larger push in education at the level of policy to simplify schooling to that which solves for the problem of the student. In that space where a great deal of borrowing happens from corporate strategizing, a focus on the koan in lieu of real pursuit of the trouble of education and its inherent discontents means we end up inundated with wordplay that eliminates complexity. We play in that space just a bit here, as Adam has presaged, in an attempt to open up a more fulsome response to what it means to teach as a matter of respect, care, and complexity. We remain, then, curious and in good company going forward.

On Weaknesses

In his book *History and Presence*, Robert Orsi (2016) writes of the inability of history as a field—and of the social sciences and humanities more broadly—to engage in good faith with the irruption of religious presence into the modern world. That is, he takes academicians to task for dismissing miracles as delusion tied to a kind of premodern and unsophisticated approach to human existence.

True presence of the holy, however, if we're to understand it as it is experienced by believers "forever exceeds the bounds set for it" (p. 29) and to set analytical constraints on faith experiences—seeking healing at holy places, experiencing God in visions, and so on—as read through the lenses of scientific empiricism is to miss the fulmination of the ways in which the "transcendent [breaks] into time" (p. 111). Indeed, Orsi continues "it may be that other domains of culture such as law, consumerism, politics, and education offer a more definite and attainable meaning and purpose than religion not only fails to provide, but actually troubles" (p. 106). Religion, in other words, can be put to work to do something unique. Which is another way of saying that limiting religion to its manifestations as a bludgeon in the culture wars is to accept terms that need not be true.

There are, Orsi (2016) proposes, different approaches to the world-as-experienced that take into account the possibility of "abundant events" (p. 67) as they restructure time, emotion, indeed life itself. Given that Britzman (1995) suggests that one of the approaches to queer theory is its study of limits, it's worth thinking at the end of the text here, about the limits of what is thinkable in teacher education vis-à-vis religious discourses. For in feminist theory, Gallop's (2002) exorbitant event, the anecdote, has long held influence; what more might we do with an abundant event that disrupts the temporal, the epistemological, the coming into the presence of, well, the presence of the divine? It is a weakness of our reading, in other words, if we fail to take up religious critiques of empiricism even as they develop very much in queer directions, simply because we as a field in teacher education mostly fail to find ourselves in religious texts along our research journey. This is, of course, ironic for anyone whose research journey takes them through thinkers like Derrida, Foucault, Badiou, Butler, West, and Dewey, who each, in different ways, engage theological and/ or religious texts. Consider, as well, for instance, the chiasmus of Butler's (2010) "precariousness as a shared condition of human life" with Bentley Hart's (2013) reflection on the nature of being as a manifestation of God in the world:

> All finite things are always, in the present, being sustained in existence by conditions that they cannot have supplied for themselves, and that together compose a universe that, as a *physical* reality, lacks the obviously supernatural power necessary to exist on its own. Nowhere in any of that is a source of existence as such. (p. 105)

It's not that we have to accept that some immovable mover is sustaining existence so much as we might consider the kinds of shared discursive conditions that make certain lives grievable in a given, inequitable circumstance as read through religious lenses. Discourse need not be reduced to God, but God is one way to understand discourse.

One way to think with this work is to move from logic to poetics. Caputo (2006) suggests a difference rooted in considerations of impossibility. He notes that "in the logic of impossibility, the impossible is simply something that cannot be, whereas in a poetics of the impossible, we are hailing an event that is otherwise than being" (p. 104). This might seem like language games, but of course, what are the queer and poststructural if not concerned with the pliability of existence in the face of signs and signifiers? What Caputo means, in reflection on his theological intervention, is that logic addresses that which is "modally possible, whereas a poetics is always a grammar of the 'perhaps'" (p. 105). That is to say that between the miraculous and the mundane there is a plane of the transcendent, whereby the former can erupt into the latter, perhaps. This resonates, of course, with work we've already cited, from Britzman through Freud, regarding the impossibility of teaching teacher education. It may, in fact, be impossible to teach teachers, in which case, if we live in a logical space, we might as well stop trying. The perhaps, in which we most likely live in any event in the field, allows for a way forward. And the field itself then, might just rest on religious foundations after all, even though we wish it might not.

The crux of Caputo's (2006) work, using Derrida, is to suggest that God, properly understood, is merely "an invitation," which is a "weak force" (p. 15) that lives at the interstices of "what disturbs being from within" (p. 9). This approach allows him to work back through Hebrew and Christian scriptures to find that "God has chosen the queer things of this earth to confound the straight and manifest his glory" (p. 201). We don't need to believe in the dogmatic sense to think about glory here so much as to understand that a shift to thinking about God as a force for weakness invites a rebuttal to the kinds of systematic theologies that most often condemn queerness. Theology, if it comes from a god who, rather than providing disorder, emerges in the cracks of existence as proof of the very disjunctive function of being and becoming and is primarily about a poetics of the perhaps at the fissures. To think with the impossible in teacher education, then, would be at least in one instantiation to think with theology toward a new poetics of the perhaps. We choose to close in this manner as we see it as fundamental to accompaniment.

Marcela Althaus-Reid's (2000) *Indecent Theology: Theological Perversions in Sex, Gender and Politics* is foundational to the field of queer theology. She begins with the assertion that "every theological discourse is implicitly a sexual discourse" (p. 23) and proposes that those discourses made most popular by major religions are decent, structured, and violently opposed to the lives of humans as they actually emerge in the world. And although we might come to her work for sentences that ring like "lust and love, and lust and justice do come together. No hymen separates them" (p. 67), we ought to tarry for her analysis that suggests that, for instance, the very presence of Mary in Christianity—the virgin, the mother of God, the human person—is queer where queerness is "the very essence of a denied reality" (p. 71). Using heterotopias as a spatial metaphor for the placedness and overlapping discourses in sexual lives, she notes that "the point of doing theology from people's experiences and from their sexual stories" is that they "reveal the falsity of the border limits between the material and divine dimension of our lives" (p. 148). Sex can be, if we attend to its pleasure rather than its shame, an example of the irruption of God into the world just as it might be the overlapping space of knowledge and pleasure, which isn't to idealize sex that is, she rightly notes, deeply human and unclean (not a value judgment as rendered in her work) and, well, visceral by definition. It's more than yelling, "Oh God," during sex, but this is a call not to skim over that tendency.

For our purposes as this intersects with teacher education, we think about the instance of the "encounter to be found at the crossroads of desire" (Althaus-Reid, 2000, p. 200) as a project of reclamation in education. There are erotic entanglements in our work as educators, and we most often don't have a language for understanding their roots other than through pathology. Althaus-Reid suggests another route, indecency, linked with, from our understanding, accompaniment. We think of this in contrast to language that pervades in education around accommodation. Accommodation arises from and settles in language and law around ability, and although our intention is not to denigrate the very necessary work of colleagues in special education for whom accommodation is vital in the service of students, we do want to think about the difference between a field that accommodates students and one that accompanies them. That finds, in encounters with students, a desire to move with them through the world rather than to move them through on their own. This is, as well, true when we think about debates about religious accommodations from antidiscrimination laws that, while legally important, frame the issues in ways that we worry don't adequately address what happens in encounters in classrooms. Accompaniment may provide time to come to understanding and into presence within education as students and teachers meet to make meaning of the world.

Sages, Guides, and Meddlers, Oh My!

One particularly popular model for conceptualizing the teacher in relation to students posits three orientations: the sage-on-the-stage, the guide-on-the-side, and the meddler-in-the-middle. Each of these, in their own way, names a role that the teacher holds (sage, guide, meddler) in relation to the student (in front of, to the side of, in the middle of). Teachers and students relate to one another based not only on the role they occupy but also on how that role plays out in the space of the classroom. Furthermore, the dynamic between them creates different conditions for different types of learning in different spatial setups. No one model can capture all the things that education can offer over the course of any individual student's life. We occupy different spaces in relation to different teachers. Rather, it is the experience of teachers and their mani-festation of these models in classrooms within students' lives through which diverse educational outcomes and experiences are achieved. Or, put differently, we think these models point toward different components of a good educa-tion that touch on engagement with knowledge (sage), experience (guide), and risk-taking (meddler) through spatial metaphors. They also emerge amid dif-ferent times and economic models: the sage, a remnant of ancient patriarchal economies; the guide, a product of modernity and the industrial age; and the meddler, a creation of postmodernism and the information age.[1] While there are cases to be made for privileging one model over another, we think the time of school is such that the diverse array of roles and positions in combination opens up opportunities since schools remain a rather strange space where ancient, industrial, and information-age ideas swirl around one another.

We suspect that the "meddler-in-the-middle," as the most recent conceptu-alization, needs a bit further explanation before we move on to accompaniment. Erica McWilliams (2008) drawing on Bauman's "liquid-modern" social world, sought to recognize the pedagogical implications of an "unfixed" reality through the figure of the meddler. For her, this asks that learning dispositions be rethought such that "educators will spend less time explaining through instruction and more time in experimental and error-welcoming modes of en-gagements" (p. 265). The meddler-in-the-middle, for McWilliams, spends more time doing the following:

1. Being a usefully ignorant co-worker
2. Being an experimenter and risk-taker
3. Being a designer, editor, and assembler
4. Being a collaborative critic and authentic evaluator. (p. 265)

These changes in being are not simple as they add another layer and set of options to consider when teaching amidst our "liquid modernity." The meddler-in-the-middle does not operate from a wise position at the front of the class, nor do they merely guide students to some destination from the side. Instead, the meddler meddles amid swiftly changing technological landscapes. In the mid-dle of students as they engage the issues at hand, the teacher refuses the position of expert, instead taking risks and experimenting with students to create space for creation and its failures. Meddling, however, is not without responsibility as the teacher collaborates with students to critique the work and evaluate such work authentically.

The meddler-in-the-middle approach recognizes the evolving realities that students and teachers face together in which large-scale challenges lie ahead: racial reckonings, global climate catastrophe, misinformation amid the quotidian—has the attendance been submitted? And while those large-scale challenges lie ahead, we (should) learn about and through such challenges within, in part, schools. In this book, we have not taken on those large-scale challenges so much as sought to contemplate a smaller challenge that happens in classrooms: the challenge of when sexuality and gender intersect with religion. More often than not, we hear of these moments as irruptions whereby student bodies and beliefs butt up against one another, leaving unprepared educators unsure how to proceed. To proceed, we want to argue, in bringing this book to a close, that our argument is not merely to teach teachers, student teachers, and teacher educators "good theology" to counter "bad theology." Such a move is clearly ensconced in matters of fact when, as Bruno Latour (2004) argues, facts fail to correct the matters at hand. As he argues,

> it has been a long time, after all, since intellectuals were in the vanguard. Indeed, it has been a long time since the very notion of the avant-garde—the proletariat, the artistic—has passed away, pushed aside by other forces, moved to the rear guard, or maybe lumped with the baggage train. (p. 226)

In that light then, Latour wonders: "Can we devise another powerful descriptive tool that deals this time with matters of concern and whose import then will no longer be to debunk but to protect and to care?" (p. 232) It concerns us that as students and teachers meet amid the complex realities they bring to the classroom, we have few ways to encounter concerns that are raised as religious beliefs mesh with experiences of sexuality and gender identity. It concerns us further that when such encounters are raised, they are most often rooted in antagonisms that capture only a part of the broader theological beliefs that frame issues around bodies and pleasures.

Accompaniment

We propose then thinking about the work and time of accompaniment. Accompaniment we hesitantly offer as a way to not replace the previously discussed models but to redefine their relationship to time. We might, in reference to the sage/meddler/guide triptych, suggest the teacher as "Companion in Class," whereby the teacher exists as a companion, a travel companion, so to speak, who moves alongside students without a predetermined spatial position. Teachers, as they travel, may very well take up the role of the sage or the guide or the meddler in any given moment. But it is the way in which they take up these roles that we are interested in such that teachers, as they share wisdom from the stage or guide students through a problem or meddle in the middle of an experiment, do so recognizing the need for the time of accompaniment.

This accompaniment is not focused solely on the student or the teacher but as students and teachers meet amid the challenging conditions to address the matters of concern that, well, concern them in time.

There are, to be clear, still power dynamics and related critical issues in play since we cannot escape those realities. Accompaniment asks that we take seriously the time it takes for those we accompany to make meaning, to learn about what is, to work to transform what could be. Accompaniment alongside does not overcome those realities but, instead, focuses on renewing the potentials that emerge as people meet, remembering, as Arendt (1954/2006) taught us, that,

> education is the point at which we decide whether we love the world
> enough to assume responsibility for it and by the same token save
> it from that ruin, which except for renewal, except for the coming
> of the new and young, would be inevitable. (p. 193)

The renewal of a common world is a never-ending task that is reborn with "the coming of the new and young." But the young cannot, as earlier noted by Arendt (1954/2006), be left to "their own devices," nor have the opportunity to undertake something new struck from their hands (p. 193). Rather, the work of education is deciding to "prepare them in advance for the task of renewing a common world" (p. 193). Such preparation is clearly a challenging task as teachers and teacher educators have to make meaning of what that looks like in practice as they encounter not only their own investments but the flesh-and-blood students in their classrooms as well.

We moved, as explained earlier, to the side of love to the work of like. We think about liking because liking, we suspect, allows for forms of accompaniment that don't define in advance where "we" are going. A good guide, after all, always knows how to get to the destination while our current circumstances are less sure about where we need to go and how to get there. Accompaniment is, in part, rooted in accompanying. To accompany is to go somewhere with someone as a companion. This may, of course, involve being a wise companion or a guide when lost or meddling, but each of those forms of being are undertaken not in a manner of asserting dominance over but accompanying alongside in ways that assist the student coming into presence in their own unique way. Such accompaniment, we suspect, might do well grappling with the paradoxes and conundrums that arise when people meet. These include, like we have explored throughout this book, the work of consideration, forgiveness, and reconciliation alongside being mindful of not being lulled into the certainty of prophetic indictment. Accompaniment cannot necessarily offer easy answers but, in its time, can assist in responding to the contingent questions and needs that arise in the scenes of schooling that may, in moments, be educative.

It might be useful to think of this in musical terms. Accompaniment, musically, means, roughly, rhythmic support of the melody: It is integral to the larger piece as it emerges but often in a supportive role. This isn't to say that the work of accompaniment means a subverting or lessening of the value of teaching. Quite the opposite, in fact. The function of accompaniment, musically, is to strengthen a given piece at the same time that it cannot be extricated from that piece without radically altering the shape of the experience. It is foundational just as it is functionally supportive. In this sense, we think of accompanying students on their journey as they come to consider issues around the intersection of religion and sexuality as necessary and catering to the particular melodies emerging from the student experience. In some cases, this will mean rebutting dangerous ideas, but it will mean doing so in a language that rhymes: In some cases, dissonance can be accompaniment too, of course, but what we're arguing for is an understanding of the rhythm that would be necessary to guide, meddle in, and/or wisely perform different possibilities being attentive to the complex array of ways such things are done.

An Ethical Imperative

We move to the side of love and hate toward liking, in part, because within Catholic conversations love has often, when it comes to homosexuality and gender nonconformity particularly, been weaponized. Catholics and many other Christians have long been told, figuratively and literally, to "love the sinner, hate the sin." This pithy saying is one that has been challenged politically through secular arguments and theologically through an array of approaches. Such challenges have, we suggest, made headway while also encountering backlash. This headway and backlash, of course, are often at the level of institutional-speak, leaving the work on the ground more complicated but also more open to care.

Think here of Pope Francis's oft-praised question "Who am I to Judge?" when asked about gay priests alongside his condemnation of "gender ideology" and the Congregation for the Doctrine of the Faith's statement against blessing same-sex unions. The mixed messages are, we suspect, a sign of the messaging needing to be remixed but also the challenges that emerge in such a process. Such a process is, we find, so polarized that rarely do the different sides meet to talk, making challenging the work of accompanying one another in making meaning for this time, now.

Accompaniment may, at first blush, sound overly romantic or perhaps just simplistic. Given the serious political, legislative, and judicial challenges that are underway asserting a form of religious liberty, or what Corvino (2017) terms religious preference, accompaniment may be nothing more than leading the lambs to the slaughter. The disproportionate impact LGBTQ+ people and communities bear as a result of such challenges cannot be understated. We are, to put it bluntly, in for a bumpy ride, but that bumpy ride need not fall along the old battle lines that pit religious discourses and communities against LGBTQ+ discourses and communities. One concern, as we close, emerges from a caution we raised early in the book: We do not wish to flatten the disproportional precarity as it exists in the world. Thomas Edsall (2021) uses the work of Johanna Ray Vollhardt to distinguish between the experiences of groups whose collective victimhood was a result of their having been objectively and systemically targeted from those groups whose victimhood emerges from a newfound threat of status loss. Vollhardt calls the latter of the two "imagined victimhood." We don't disagree, and we certainly understand the difference between LGBTQ+ individuals who have suffered and continue to suffer at the hands of a religiously resonant approach to sexuality in society and those Christians among us who experience this current moment of supposed secularism as a violent loss. Our point, and this is where accompaniment is perhaps most useful, is that both groups of students (among many other groups, of course) are present with us in the teacher education classroom. The main question is, What we do, pedagogically, with humans coming into presence who, among other experiences, view themselves reasonably or not, as victims of oppression in the world? Theology offers us a different kind of harmonic support for our students across the broad spectrum of humanity and its sexualities; we just need to do the work of finding our voice anew.

Finding our voice anew inevitably means being willing to risk the self and the comforts of our knowledge. It means being willing to let go of cherished ideas and ideals amid the ever-present need for questioning. As Maxine Greene (1995) taught us,

> by becoming aware of ourselves as questioners, as makers of meaning, as persons engaged in constructing and reconstructing realities with those around us, we may be able to communicate to students the notion that reality depends on perspective, that its construction is never complete, and that there is always more. (p. 382)

There is always more that asks that we continue to be open to the work of teacher education as it encounters the work of students coming into presence, struggling through this process amid the work of becoming a teacher. Can teacher educators accompany student teachers through this process, recognizing the time it takes to become a teacher while remembering that student teachers are, like teacher educators, always already in scenes of learning about themselves and others? Can we learn to like others as a part of this process in ways that don't predetermine who or what students should become? We remain curious to accompany you in seeking answers to these questions.

Endnotes

1 Special thanks to John Neff for his help in thinking through the spatial and economic roots of these models of teaching.

References

Alison, J. (2003). *On being liked*. Herder & Herder.

Althaus-Reid, M. (2000). *Indecent theology: Theological perversions in sex, gender and politics*. Routledge.

Arendt, H. (2006). The crisis in education. In *Between Past and Future* (pp. 170–193). Penguin. (Original work published 1954).

Britzman, D. (1995). Is there a queer pedagogy? Or, stop reading straight. *Educational Theory, 45*(2), 151-165.

Butler, J. (2010). *Frames of war: When is life grievable?* Verso.

Caputo, J. D. (2006). *The weakness of God: A theology of the event.* Indiana University Press.

Corvino, J., Anderson, R. T., & Girgis, S. (2017). *Debating religious liberty and discrimination.* Oxford University Press.

Edsall, T. B. (2021, April 21). Why Trump is still their guy. *New York Times.* https://www.nytimes.com/2021/04/21/opinion/trump-republicans.html

Gallop, J. (2002). *Anecdotal theory.* Duke University Press.

Greene, M. (1995). Art and imagination: Reclaiming the sense of possibility. *The Phi Delta Kappan, 76*(5), 378–382.

Hart, D. B. (2013). *The experience of God: Being, consciousness, bliss.* Yale University Press.

Latour, B. (2004). Why has critique run out of steam? From matters of fact to matters of concern. *Critical Inquiry, 30*(2), 225–248.

McWilliams, E. (2008). Unlearning to teach. *Innovations in Education and Teaching International, 45*(3), 263–269.

Orsi, R. A. (2016). *History and presence.* Harvard University Press

Sell, J., & Reiss, M. J. (2020). Faith-sensitive RSE in areas of low religious observance: Really? *Sex Education.* Advanced online publication. https://doi.org/10.1080/14681811.2020.1835634

About The Authors

Kevin J. Burke, PhD, is an associate professor in the Department of Language and Literacy Education and an affiliate faculty member of Interdisciplinary Qualitative Studies as well as in the Institute for Women's Studies at the University of Georgia. He teaches courses on masculinities, queer theory, religion, and public education, as well as on the practice of and evaluation in community-based youth-centered literacy research. His most recent books include *Culturally Sustaining Systemic Functional Linguistic Praxis: Embodied Inquiry in Youth Art Spaces,* coauthored with Ruth Harman (Routledge, 2020), and *Legacies of Christian Languaging and Literacies in American Education: Perspectives on English Language Arts Curriculum, Teaching, and Learning,* coedited with Mary Juzwik, Jennifer Stone, and Denise Davila (Routledge, 2019).

Adam J. Greteman, PhD, is an associate professor in the Department of Art Education at the School of the Art Institute of Chicago. His teaching and research interests lie at the intersections of feminist, queer, and transgender theories; the philosophy of education; aesthetics; and art education. He is a cofounder (with Karen Morris, Nic Weststrate, and Todd Williams) of the LGBTQ+ Intergenerational Dialogue Project. His work has been published in *QED: A Journal of Queer Worldmaking, Sex Education,* the *Journal of Homosexuality,* and *Educational Theory.* He is the author of the award-winning *Sexualities and Genders in Education: Toward Queer Thriving* (Palgrave Macmillan, 2018) and the coauthor, with Kevin J. Burke, of *The Pedagogies and Politics of Liking* (Routledge, 2017).

INDEX